Exotic Style

GREAT IDEAS FOR BRINGING GLOBAL STYLE HOME **SARA BLISS**

GLOUCESTER MASSACHUSETTS

ROCKPORT PUBLISHERS

First published in the United States of America by
Rockport Publishers, Inc.
33 Commercial Street
Gloucester, Massachusetts 01930-5089
Telephone: (978) 282-9590
Facsimile: (978) 283-2742
www.rockpub.com

ISBN 1-56496-862-6

10 9 8 7 6 5 4 3 2 1

Design: Yee Design
Cover Image: ©Red Cover/Ken Hayden
Back Cover: Reprinted by Permission from *House Beautiful*, copyright ©
July, 1998. Hearst Communications, Inc. All Rights Reserved. Nedjeljko
Matura, photographer, left; Reprinted by Permission from *House Beautiful*,
copyright © March, 1998. Hearst Communications, Inc. All Rights Reserved.
Alexandre Bailhache, photographer, middle; Courtesy of Zimmer + Rohde,
Textile manufacturers of three different lines: Ardecora, Etamine, and
Zimmer + Rohde, right

Photo Research: Wendy Missan
Special thanks to *House Beautiful* and *Veranda*

Printed in China

Contents

INTRODUCTION ✿

On a journey around the world when I was ten, I became captivated with global design, food, and fashion. In every country we visited, there were new sights, sounds, tastes, smells, and styles to discover. The highlight of each city we visited was exploring the flea markets and antique shops with the anticipation of gathering new treasures to bring home. From Jakarta to Hong Kong, these vibrant marketplaces offered nonstop intrigue with beautifully crafted goods and fabrics, each one more stunning than the last. My favorite find was the bazaar in Istanbul, a magical place where seemingly endless corridors were lined with stalls that sold infinite treasures, from watercolors to carpets and clothing.

It was there that I fell in love with exotic design and was fascinated by patterns, styles, and creations I had never before imagined. After examining several sets of harem pants in a dozen or so shops, searching for the perfect pair and, of course, price, I settled on purple satin with gold embroidery and a matching vest. I learned the fine art of bargaining, joyfully haggling with the shop owners while frequently referring to my guidebook for helpful Turkish phrases. I have never forgotten that experience and the thrill of discovering something entirely new. International design continues to captivate me—the great variation of styles from region to region, the amazing craftsmanship of handmade products, and the myriad decorating choices available beyond my corner of the world.

In this book, I hope to share with you this love of global design. How to make the leap from gathering gorgeous global wares and incorporating them into your home is a major theme of *Exotic Style*. I will show you how to use international fabrics, furniture, art, and accessories the way a designer would, covering everything from how to maximize a small space to how to create a romantic boudoir. In my home growing up, my mother, an interior designer and artist, was a master at mixing a multicultural blend of pieces: in the living room, a Thai rain drum was paired with an American wingback armchair, Chinese stools, and a traditional Western beige sofa topped with mirror-inlaid Indian pillows. I hope that after reading this book you will be inspired to create your own magical mix, whether you pair English antiques with Japanese screens or batiks with 1950s American chairs.

While fusion decorating may be a hot trend in interior design, it is more than a phase; it is a new direction that is also occurring in fashion and food. The world is becoming smaller, and we should take advantage of having a wide range of aesthetic styles to influence us. No matter what your budget or taste, I hope this book will inspire you to bring the world home.

Exotic Atmospheres

Exotic tastes and objects have always fascinated Western culture. Anything new and unusual—from architecture to fabrics—has been a source of inspiration for voyagers. There is nothing new about bringing objects from other cultures into the home. As far back as the second century B.C., the Silk Road brought luxury items such as silk and jade from China to Rome. Later, in the nineteenth century, British aristocrats traveled to India, gathering furniture, rugs, and art. The Victorians were enchanted by Turkish design, and Turkish rooms were often re-created in the wealthiest homes. Exotic motifs and designs influenced not only interiors but Western art as well. For example, Picasso's fascination with African masks inspired his work, including his famous painting Les Demoiselles d'Avignon. Today, we are still obsessed with the stunning look of exotic pieces and are captivated by the joy of seeing things arranged or designed in a way that never occurred to us. ¶ Whether you're adding a few global touches or transforming entire rooms, there is a wealth of exotic design elements available. Never before has it been so easy to shop the globe. In only a matter of hours you can fly to the bazaars of Marrakesh or the open-air markets in Guatemala. Without leaving the house, you can order almost anything on-line, from Indonesian rattan furniture to Peruvian Ayacucho rugs. At flea markets, specialty shops, and on the Web, you'll find an assortment of breathtaking contemporary and antique treasures, from Turkish lanterns to Chinese stools. The best the world has to offer is right at your fingertips.

OPPOSITE: *Creating an exotic atmosphere comes from a clever mix of elements. Here, fabric-covered walls set the tone, enhanced by Turkish watercolors and a Moorish chair.*

From fusion cuisine to exotic design, the exciting thing about blending influences from around the world is in creating original, new looks and tastes. Incorporating exotic elements into your design updates a room and makes every space unique. From elegant Japanese scroll paintings to beautifully carved marble chess sets from Mexico, there is an exceptional selection of global art, games, furniture, fabrics, and decorative objects for every area of the house. Many of these items are handcrafted using techniques passed down through the ages. Contemporary designers use traditional methods to craft modern goods. Depending on your budget, you can find small accessories for a few dollars, or you can find antiques that will be major investments. Whether you enjoy collecting upscale antiques or vintage flea market finds, you will find items to fit your budget and style.

When you substitute ordinary objects with a multicultural blend of objects chosen for their unique shapes, patterns, or craftsmanship, you are on your way to successfully designing an exotic interior. Creating an exotic atmosphere starts by adding a few unexpected surprises to a room— replacing that boring glass coffee table with a weathered Indian drum or exchanging a framed museum poster for a dazzling beaded and metal-

lic embroidered Nigerian George fabric. Designing a global interior is about making practical household pieces stand out by selecting unusual global treasures in lieu of machine-made mass-produced goods. Start with small global accents that delight the eye and give a room pizzazz. Add exotic pieces to every room in the house, from your bathroom to your kitchen.

There are many ways to incorporate global items into your home design. You can create an exotic mood with color, textiles, furniture, art, flowers, and accessories. Try adding color influenced by another part of the world, or redesign your entire place with global furniture, or simply bring in a few little accents here and there. If you love one type of object, then become a collector. For instance, if you enjoy exotic lighting, let global lights set the mood in every room: add the sexy glow of a henna-painted lantern to a bedroom, or place a whimsical lamp crafted from a Chinese hat box in a child's room. There are no rules; just enjoy the many options that you have to choose from. The key to creating an exotic atmosphere is to combine and juxtapose East with West and North with South—and never ever be limited by one look.

Color

From muted to vibrant, colors carry deep personal and cultural significance. Around the world, color is symbolic, expressing a range of distinctive and deeply held beliefs. For instance, in China, red is associated with power and good fortune, but in India, red is the color of love and sensuality. Color can also make a defining statement, setting a look and mood for a particular culture.

As you learn about architecture, art, and design associated with different parts of the globe, you will relate various hues and palettes as well. The soft green of a jade carving can remind you of China, and the crisp white rice paper of a Shoji screen becomes representative of Japan. Vibrant orange and hot pink evoke colors found in northern India. A Kente cloth's powerful combination of yellows, green, black, and red is expressive of Ghana. Crisp, white stucco will bring you back to Greece, and white houses with red roofs will remind you of Mexico. The timeless combination of indigo and white in a batik is an example of fresh Indonesian style.

Ultimately, color is very personal. A global home is filled with shades that remind you of wonderful travels and make every space sing. Use color freely whether you re-create the dazzling hues of Mexico or the warm tones of Nigeria. Take your cues from the application of color in houses, clothes, furniture, and fabrics around the world. Study international carpets, antique textiles, and paintings to learn about timeless color combinations or unexpected palettes and then bring those hues home.

Try these palettes to capture an exotic atmosphere in your space. Accent any color with black or gold for an exotic feel.

Using Exotic Colors at Home

*Looking to add global glamour to your place? Take advantage of vibrant hues and gorgeous patterns from around the world. Fabric designer, artist, and designer **Lulu de Kwiatkowski** offers inspiration on **combining exotic color**:*

Use colors from around the world to inspire you. **Every region has its color** and, if done right, anything can be adapted to an interior. Japan has a honey orange, and China has Mother Earth's answer to red. India has a pale faded indigo, Spain has a golden yellow, Cuba has a salmon pink, and Italy has an enviable polished ivory.

The best starting point when **creating a color palette** for a room is to choose an object with a great sense of color, such as an embroidered pillow, a great rug, or a vase. Work around the object's palette. Pull out the main colors, and use them as highlights throughout your space.

When **painting a space** always throw a dash of cappuccino color into whatever hue you use. Pale blues, greens, and yellows look sterile if they are not softened a bit.

All colors should be combined with natural earth tones—browns, beiges, and creams, so that hues will mesh as they do in nature. If you're nervous about using color just choose one or two, and pair them with earthy shades.

When choosing fabrics and furniture **mix different styles**—but it has to flow. Too many extremes can jolt the eye. You have to go with you instinct. If your instinct is throwing you off one day, simple clean lines are always safest.

Bathe walls in a globally inspired color, like these rich luminous squares. The color is inspired by Japanese and Chinese lacquer painted by artist Lulu de Kwiatkowski.

Fabric

From the sizzling stripes of Guatemalan textiles to the graphic combinations of brown shades in Kuba cloth, there is a sensational selection of handmade global fabrics. Age-old techniques produce appliquéd, embroidered, beaded, block-printed, woven, or resist-dyed textiles crafted by the skilled hand and discerning eye of an artisan. From a tie-dyed silk Bandhani cloth from India to a cotton Ewe cloth from Ghana, many traditional methods of crafting fabrics are still practiced today and cannot be mimicked with machines. Every handcrafted fabric is an original, time-intensive work of art. Bring handmade textiles to your home for an original look.

LEFT: *For fabrics with a modern vibe, collect pieces with graphic patterns—from bold stripes to abstract designs, such as these hand-woven fabrics from Senegal. Design by Claire Beaumont.*

OPPOSITE: *Gather an unrelated mix of lively and intricate global fabrics in an assortment of materials, patterns, and colors to make eye-catching pillows and cushions.*

Bringing Exotic Fabrics Home

*Whether you're searching for radiantly colorful silks, crisp linens, or vintage embroidered cottons, there are millions of incredibly enticing global textiles for you to choose from. What to do with your eye-catching fabrics when you bring them home? Textile Designer **John Robshaw**, who produces fabrics employing age-old techniques in India, Thailand, and Indonesia, offers some suggestions on decorating with ethnic textiles:*

✦

Learn about how specific textiles were traditionally used—perhaps they were made for temple decorations, as room dividers, or wedding sarongs—then **be creative** and use them in your own way.

Use richly colored **Indian saris** as window panels. Saris measure approximately 5 yards by 44 inches (4.6 m by 112 cm). Throw one over a curtain rod so it becomes a flat panel, or wrap one around the rod as a window dressing. Another option is to hang two to form more traditional curtains.

In Indonesia, locals wear **Batik sarongs**, but sarongs are also the perfect size for a festive (and washable) tablecloth. The exquisite hand-drawn batiks also look amazing as art, hung flat on a wall.

Try covering a set of dining chairs with antique **Thai silks**. Each chair will be unique, but the patterns, colors, and material will complement each other.

Embroidered **Laos shawls** are the perfect length to go across a dining room table for a gorgeous tablerunner.

Gents **wool shawls** from **India** come in brown, gray, and cream and can be wrapped as shawls on cold nights, as they do in Delhi, or used as warm blankets or throws.

When you are **hunting for fabrics abroad**, always ask the locals where to buy fabrics, and don't miss the bazaars and outdoor markets. In India you can visit sari shops and find hundreds of beautiful designs.

ABOVE: *In John Robshaw's studio in New York he's gathered a lively mix of his designs crafted in Southeast Asia including colorful vegetable dyed block printed textiles, and indigo dyed resist printed fabrics, and batiks.*

OPPOSITE: *John Robshaw Textile designs, mixed with antique textiles from his collection, adorn a Long Island barn. The exotic hues feel right at home in this classic American setting.*

B atik is a resist-printing process that originated in Indonesia. It produces exuberantly patterned fabrics. Modern batiks come in a range of vivid colors and exude a tropical mood that can effortlessly jazz up even the dullest interior. The cotton or silk fabrics work perfectly for pillows, tablecloths, wall hangings, napkins, shirts, or sarongs.

MAKING A BATIK

1. Artisans begin by drawing designs with a pencil on beige or white silk or cotton.

2. Hot wax is applied with a penlike wax holder called a canting or a patterned copper stamp called a cap. The wax resists the dye and creates the design. Patterns tend to be repeating geometric designs or freeform motifs inspired by nature.

3. The cloth is dipped in a dye vat—quickly for a lighter shade or longer for deeper color. Originally, natural dyes produced blue, brown, and red colors, but in the 1850s the introduction of chemical dyes provided an endless choice of hues.

4. When the cloth is removed from the dye, wax is scraped off with a knife and hot water.

5. For multicolored and more intricate designs, this process is repeated and the wax is applied to different areas.

TRADITIONAL USE OF BATIKS

In Indonesia batiks are used as clothing. Batik sarongs, worn by both men and women, are rectangular pieces of fabric that are wrapped around the waist and tied or folded to form a skirt. In more rural areas it is common to see women tying sarongs around their bodies and using the fabric as baby carriers. A more recent and very popular introduction is the Western-style batik shirt worn by men since independence from the Dutch.

USING BATIKS TODAY

The spectacularly intricate designs of batik fabrics can add tropical flair to an apartment, or dress up a hostess at a pool party. Batiks are usually cottons and silks, so they work best as accent fabrics rather than upholstery. Here are some ideas for living with batiks:

Tie one on. Batik sarongs make chic cover-ups at the pool as well as a stylish beach blanket.

Set the table. Many sarongs are large enough to use as tablecloths for an outdoor soiree.

Board it up. Cover a bulletin board with a favorite batik print. Allow 1 inch extra all around, pull the fabric tight, and staple the material to the back.

Punctuate. Mix and match patterns for a medley of exotic and colorful floor or throw pillows.

Hang them up. Many antique batiks are time-intensive works of art—hang one on the wall as you would a painting. Another option is to frame small pieces of vintage fabrics; a group of three or more will look terrific when displayed on a wall.

Exotic Goods

When you're designing a space, look for chairs, tables, lighting, and carpets that capture an exotic mood. From the romantic curves of a wicker and rattan daybed crafted in Java to the festive hues of Indian sari fabric, every element you select for a room changes the overall dynamic. Let every space tell a story about your travels, even if they're just jaunts to the local flea market. Whether you just add one amazing exotic piece or a multicultural mix of objects, you'll be creating unique personal spaces.

When you're shopping for new things, look for unusual and one-of-a-kind elements that add character to a room—from rare tribal art to Pre-Columbian sculpture. If you have a lot of basic pieces, global accents are just the thing to breathe new life into a predictable room. If you already have lots of color and pattern, look for pieces with interesting shapes and textures to balance out a space. The secret to designing fabulous rooms with global items is to choose elements that enhance the pieces you already have. Look at what's missing in your rooms. Are they lacking in color, texture, pattern, or original designs? Then find stunning exotic accents to fill those gaps.

ABOVE: *Art and sculpture provide the finishing touches for every room. A praying Buddhist sculpture sets a reflective mood in this London living room.*

OPPOSITE: *Replace boring light fixtures with handcrafted global lighting, such as this inexpensive, delicately painted and tasseled mesh Chinese lantern.*

Shopping for Exotic Accents

There are many places where you can find international goods, from the outdoor markets in Hong Kong to your laptop. Close to home, one of the easiest places to start is at a reputable auction house. Today, they carry everything from tribal art to Chinese antiquities.

Auction houses are wonderful places to begin learning about international antiques. The major houses produce color catalogs with detailed information about different pieces of furniture and sculpture. Going to an auction preview is an ideal way to educate yourself about exotic furniture, since unlike at a museum, you can handle objects, and specialists are on hand to answer any questions. Another great resource are reputable dealers and importers, who often carry various categories of items—classified by country of origin, type of object, or age—and always seem eager to share their knowledge. When purchasing an antique, make sure you only do business with well-established dealers.

The Internet is a lively global marketplace. Many new Web sites that specialize in handcrafted items from around the world have been getting a lot of attention. Apply the same rules for shopping on the Web as you do for shopping at traditional stores. Always buy from established businesses that offer you written guarantees and a good return policy in

LEFT: *A timeless favorite of collectors, Chinese blue-and-white porcelain, shown here in a Blue Canton pattern, comes in every imaginable shape and size. Design by Mottahedeh.*

OPPOSITE:
Choose furniture that makes a statement, such as this antique Chinese cabinet with stunning architectural lines.

case your treasures are not exactly what you thought you ordered. Or shop from Web sites that are linked with brick-and-mortar businesses that have been established for several years. Shipping is often the tricky and expensive part of shopping the Web, so make sure you are getting a fair deal and that the shipper has insurance to cover any shipping damage.

For fun and often inexpensive shopping, explore flea markets. It helps to go with someone who knows about global pieces and what prices they should fetch. If you are buying inexpensive pieces such as baskets, there isn't anything to worry about; however, if you are investing in major pieces of furniture that are costly or over one hundred years old, make sure you protect yourself. The same is true for bazaars and flea markets abroad, which are often the most lively and exciting places to shop around the world. You get a true sense of local life, tastes, smells, and sights from roaming around these markets. If you are buying abroad, go with someone who speaks the language to get the best prices—and always bargain!

Display

Show off your discerning eye with powerful displays that spotlight your global treasures. Often people who are collectors make the mistake of buying things and then hiding them away until they have use for them; don't let your exotic goods drown in a sea of clutter or place objects in a corner where they can be easily overlooked. Always carve out space for display on your walls, bureaus, tabletops, mantles, and shelves.

If you are exhibiting a random assortment of objects, such as an interesting scroll painting, a jade sculpture, an antique Syrian appliquéd textile, and Indonesian masks, place them in various parts of the house so they don't compete with one another. For example, highlight the jade sculpture on a

shelf by itself, place the scroll painting above a mantle, frame the textile in an attention-grabbing frame, and line the masks together along one wall. Don't group a hodgepodge of objects together simply because they are exotic elements, spotlight each item by exhibiting it in a special place where it will be noticed.

If you collect specific types of objects and art, such as netsuke, international bells, or Japanese teapots, group them together for a powerful composition. Arrange objects by color or type for a modern, clean arrangement. If you love textiles, fold various fabrics according to color and pattern in open shelving or in baskets. Being able to see the textiles you've gathered may spark some ideas for how to use them. If you collect dishes, create a plate rack on shelves to show them off, or hang them on walls. For a collection of pottery or sculpture, arrange groupings on tabletops, sideboards or armoires. If you have an abundance of exciting tableware, such as colorful Mexican glassware or unusual African serving pieces, show them off on open shelves in the kitchen or arranged prominently in a display case. Rare coins, colorful stamps, or other small collections should be framed and hung together for maximum impact. Whether you like collecting vases, sculpture, framed prints, or baskets, present your collections in a way that celebrates their style.

LEFT: *Display similar objects in groups for a striking effect.*

OPPOSITE: *Exhibit favorite collections prominently. Here open shelves provide a home for a variety of baskets.*

Shopping for Global Goods

*Be a savvy global shopper! Knowing what to expect before you buy items abroad can make the trip even better. Boston's Mohr & McPherson specializes in importing and selling an international collection of furniture, accessories, and antiques. Owner **Kevin McPherson** shares his do's and don'ts on **buying items from around the world**.*

Do buy antique exotic furniture for a good investment. Often an item will sell for a reasonable price when first discovered by the American and European markets, but as supply diminishes, the item may quickly become a collectible and will increase in value.

Do buy from as direct a source as possible when shopping for global objects in the United States to ensure the best price.

Do trust your own taste and don't worry whether global pieces will go with your existing furniture. If you buy what you like, your home will look like the home of a collector instead of having the static look of an unimaginative decorator's work.

Do buy pieces from established businesses with several years experience and a good reputation. Just because someone gives you a certificate of authenticity doesn't mean it is always valid.

Do have a thorough knowledge of the export laws concerning antiques from the country you are buying from. Some countries put a limit on the age of an item able to be exported.

Don't place orders to have furniture custom-made overseas. You may receive a final product that is very different than your original specifications.

Don't buy wood furniture in the tropics because the wood will have absorbed a great deal of moisture. When it lands in the United States and is exposed to central heat and air conditioning, it will crack and warp.

The difference between buying here and abroad is profound. When you buy furniture overseas, the customer almost always absorbs the costs for any problems with the merchandise.

Finishing a Room

Finishing touches add spark to your rooms. Whether it's the subtle detail of a hand-painted porcelain doorknob, a collection of Chinese brush pots, or a cedar picture frame from El Salvador, distinctive decorative accents finalize a room. Every element adds to the overall style of a space, so don't overlook even the smallest accessory or detail. Incorporate exotic elements, motifs, and accessories with your own design. One inexpensive idea is to enhance a basic piece of furniture with paint, pattern, and hardware. For instance, take an ordinary wood chest of drawers, and paint or stencil a motif inspired by a global pattern, such as an Indian fabric or a mosaic tile floor. Then, replace traditional brass drawer-pulls with international hand-crafted ones, such as ornate iron pulls from Mexico. The result is a dazzling exotic treasure that was created simply by adding a few decorative touches.

Since every detail makes a difference in the overall look of your room, try replacing items you use every day—but hardly notice—with striking substitutes. Try switching an understated wooden bookend with a Chinese stone sculpture or replacing a glass vase with a stunning Indian silver-inlay version. Select accessories that will enhance your space and set an exotic mood. Choose from global hardware, tiles, trays, frames, candles, vases, jars, or artwork. Often the finishing touches are the most personal, whether it is a collection of treasured objects or a few little things gathered here and there on trips. Look for items that are expressions of who you are and design that inspires you to finish a room beautifully and personally.

OPPOSITE: *Every detail, such as these bright hand-painted knobs and tiles, helps to create an exotic atmosphere.*

RIGHT: *Transform a low cocktail table into an Asian-inspired dining table by adding sensational silk runners to the table and surrounding it with Chinese silk pillows for seating.*

Exotic Rooms

Incorporate global design into every room for an inventive and intriguing home. Whether you simply add a lively rug or completely redecorate with a multicultural mix of furniture, global elements will ensure that each room will have its own voice. Experiment with a range of exotic styles, palettes, textiles, and furniture to give each space a look all its own. Enliven each area, no matter how small, with a stunning international detail or two. Try incorporating the exotic into your own design, such as adding a colorful landscape painting from Argentina, a striking four-poster Portuguese spool bed, or a set of Mexican glasses. When designing a room, let its purpose be your guide; make sure that each space is functional and encourages the activities that take place there. For example, your living area should have an inviting and comfortable seating area, whether you choose Indian inspired floor-level cushions and bolsters, or an arrangement of cozy sofas and chairs upholstered in African tribal fabric. ¶ Practicality doesn't have to be boring. Essentials can be offbeat and original: an antique hand-carved Peruvian wooden mirror for the bathroom, a Chinese silk bedcover for your sleeping space, or leather chairs from the Andes for the dining room. By adding an unexpected object to each room, you'll jazz up the design and create eye-catching spaces. Try incorporating a piece that is the opposite style, color, or texture of the rest of the space. For instance, soften the edges of a contemporary living area with an intricately carved and inlaid Anglo-Indian armchair or liven up a bland room by covering walls in a bold batik. Another idea is to surprise

OPPOSITE: *Global armoires, bowls, and covered containers are practical—and eye-catching.*

even the most basic and practical rooms with a purely decorative touch, such as showcasing a collection of antique Chinese pottery in a bathroom or displaying Brazilian ceramic animal sculptures in the laundry room. ❡ New palettes, styles, arrangements, and textures can be the perfect way to update a space. The key is to never get stuck in a decorating rut where you are repeating the same look in every corner of your place. Certain colors evoke different parts of the world—pink in India or cinnabar red in China. Bring those hues and palettes to your corner of the globe. Repeat the main colors of a favorite Dhurrie rug in the living room, or bathe the balcony in crisp Mediterranean blue and white. For fun, create a melange of several styles in your home. Who says an eclectic children's room can't sit next to a classic dining space? Let a sultry Moroccan bedroom or a minimalist Japanese home inspire your own design incorporating ideas from abroad in your own place. Always decorate with a range of textures, from a rough coir mat to a sexy silk for a tactile experience. Play with furniture arrangements, editing, adding, and moving everything around to see a space in an entirely new way. ❡ Mixing things up is almost always a way to refresh a room and see where some interesting global elements can be incorporated. Choose necessities that are luxurious, unusual, whimsical, or simply breathtaking, so that your rooms will celebrate the best of international design. Always give your living spaces, sleeping spaces, dining spaces, bathing spaces, and outdoor spaces a global perspective.

Exotic Living Spaces

When designing your living room, there are three important goals to keep in mind: creating a place that is comfortable, designing a space that is inviting to guests, and decorating with personal favorites that reveal something about you. Whether you prefer drama or understatement, your living space should be the room where you show off your sense of style. Bring in a few eye-catching exotic elements in lieu of basic pieces. For example, add hand-printed, bright, Indian fabric curtains in lieu of plain white ones, or scrap that traditional sideboard for an antique Japanese Tansu chest.

You do absolutely everything in your living room, including lounging, entertaining, eating, reading, watching television, working, and of course, socializing. Therefore, the overall design of the living area needs to be flexible to encourage the multitude of activities that take place there. With the popularity of loftlike open plans, the living and dining areas are often in one space rather than two. While this is a new trend in Western homes, it actually follows in the footsteps of many other countries, such as India, where relaxing, feasting, and socializing are all done in one flexible, open space. In Japan one-room living is encouraged by a lack of defining furniture. Shoji screens retract to create one big room for living and eating or slide out to partition off areas, enabling privacy and sleep. For a versatile living space, invest in multipurpose furniture such as an African Dogan stool that can be a comfy seat, an extra footstool, or a chic side table.

⸙ ✳ ⸙

ABOVE: *Create a cozy seating area with fabrics inspired by global designs and colors.*

OPPOSITE: *Use pattern to create distinct spaces within a room. Blue-and-yellow decorative tiles define this stunning seating area.*

A Little Goes a Long Way

Although the living area is often one of the largest spaces in the house, resist the impulse to pack it with furniture. More space doesn't necessarily mean you need more things! Even a large area can be overwhelmed by too much furniture and too many competing colors, patterns, and styles. Often, living rooms are dumping grounds for furniture that didn't work in other sections of the house. To avoid clutter, make sure every piece serves, a purpose either as a decorative object or as a functional one. Also, invest in furniture and accessories that provide abundant storage, so that everything has a home.

Don't hold onto an object because you think you might use it one day. If you're not using an item now, chances are you still won't be in a few years. One of the most popular pieces of advice from designers is to edit. Rearrange furniture or remove items that you haven't used in a while. This allows you to see a space with fresh eyes and decide what looks amazing and what you should unload. Often, when you look at furniture arrangements or art every day, you become immune to the eyesores and problem areas. Moving pieces around as well as editing will refresh a room.

Show restraint when you are designing a living room, especially one that will showcase global

fabrics and furniture. The focus should be on the unique treasures that you have gathered and not blurred by excess purchases. Many global items feature bold colors, graphic patterns, and unique forms that capture attention. But too many showstoppers end up competing with each other and overpowering a room. It is best to choose one or two visually powerful items that will be the focus of the space; try adding a detailed Tibetan carpet, chairs upholstered in a Turkish fabric, or a North African rolltop desk. The rest of the room should complement these treasures by echoing their colors or balancing their size and scale. For example, if you have a painted chest from India with red, greens, and yellows—try repeating the color scheme in upholstery and accessories.

ABOVE: *A well-edited room puts the spotlight on the sculptural forms of furniture, unique accessories, and luscious fabrics.*

ABOVE: *Rolling split bamboo screens, comfortable floor cushions, and low seating give this modern space an Asian-inspired flair.*

Small Spaces

Whether you live in a one-bedroom apartment or a four-bedroom house, you could probably use more space. However, the most functional rooms are not determined by how much room there is but how well the space is used. The first trick is to find multipurpose pieces that take on a new life according to your needs. Another idea is to look for exotic pieces that add lots of hidden storage. Here are a few global finds that will help you maximize the space you have:

ABOVE: *Decorative throw pillows can be easily moved to create extra seating.*

OPPOSITE: *A space-saving solution is multipurpose furniture. In a pinch, this coffee table can be transformed into a bench that accommodates an extra guest or two.*

Stools. There are many exquisite examples of hand-carved antique and contemporary Chinese and African wood stools. They can serve as attractive side tables, as well as provide sturdy seating. If you find two or three stools of the same height with flat tops, put them side-by-side to form a spacious coffee table.

Trunks. Depending on your style, there are a variety of trunks to choose from, including pretty teak trunks with carved floral motifs from India or tropical Filipino woven rattan versions. In the living room, use trunk as a coffee table. If you have a collection of trunks, stack several sizes and styles from largest to smallest against a wall. Trunks offer practical and roomy storage whether you are hiding away out of season sweaters or your toddler's toys.

Rustic benches. On the market you'll find sleek long low benches carved from one piece of wood, with some particularly stellar examples from India, West Africa, and Peru. If they are wide and relatively flat they can be used as cocktail table as well as a two-person bench. If the bench is sloped, try placing a stack of illustrated books or several folded textiles in the center.

Low tables. If your dining and living space are combined into one area, save room by making a low rectangular or square table from India, China, or Japan a living room table during the day and a dining table at night. To make the transformation from a cocktail table that pairs with a Western-style sofa to a low-level dinner table, all you need are some wide, square floor cushions for seating.

Floor pillows. Large, square floor pillows are extremely versatile. Toss them on the floor for colorful, comfortable seating or throw them on sofas, chairs, and beds. There are gorgeous ready-made pillows in every type of fabric. For elegant style look for pillows crafted from Japanese Kimonos. For a casual and summery style, try woven straw versions. Fashion your own unique floor cushions from extra or odd pieces of ethnic textiles. To keep rooms spontaneous display a multitude of pillows in a spirited assortment of textures, hues, and designs.

Screens. Exotic folding screens from all over the world including Mexico, India, China, Korea, and Japan are a superb way to divide a room. Another option is sliding paper screens from Japan. Screens are especially useful in small, multipurpose spaces. For example, if your home office is in the living room a screen can offer some privacy.

Armoires. Extremely popular export items, especially for hiding away TVs, armoires are an easy way to tuck away the clutter of everyday life. From the minimalist Chinese versions to the intricately carved armoires fashioned from antique doors in India, there are a range of options. You'll find a variety of sizes and styles complete with roomy shelves, drawers, and storage nooks to suit any space.

Bringing Global Style Home

*Shopping the globe is the fun part, but how do you pull it all together? New York designer **Roderick Shade** frequently uses international furniture and accessories in the rooms he designs. He shares his secrets for successfully **designing a global space**:*

Look everywhere. I find international items in flea markets, junk shops, and fine antique galleries. I found one of my best sources of African sculpture and baskets at a Manhattan street fair.

Edit a room before you add to it. Don't put too many pieces in one room because the space loses its focus. The hardest part about designing any great room is paring down—adding items is easy.

Stick to a theme based on a particular region or country. Decide what your ethnic influence is going to be. For a seamless look, stick to accessories from one continent or region.

Always use a really tight color scheme. Too many colors or patterns are disruptive to the eye. I like to use three basic colors and repeat, repeat, repeat. I often use a strong neutral, some white, and a dark color like dark brown, dark gray, or black.

Add small touches. Mix in ethnic accessories with traditional or contemporary furniture to create a globally influenced room that strikes the right balance between Western and ethnic design influences.

ABOVE: *A sassy mix of rustic and refined in a room designed by Roderick Shade.*

Incorporating Global Goods into Your Living Spaces

ABOVE: *Create snazzy spaces that are perfect blends of design from various parts of the globe. Here, Indian reclining teak-and-cane armchairs, an Asian bamboo table, Thai silk pillows, and Indonesian masks share the spotlight.*

Exotic accessories and furniture are so popular because people are tired of the ordinary look of mass-produced pieces. No one wants to have a room that smacks of uninspired, cookie-cutter design or looks as though you ordered everything from a catalog. Every room should have one piece that offers an element of surprise, and the handcrafted beauty of ethnic items is often just the right touch to add some spark to a room. Choosing items simply because they are handmade gems from far off lands is, however, the wrong way to go. Instead, look for pieces that are practical, exude global glamour, and complement existing furniture that you already own.

The most eye-catching exotic interiors are brilliant and brave combinations of the familiar and the foreign and are not over-the-top theme rooms. While it can be fun to design a Japanese tearoom or a Thai style dining room, tastes and trends change quickly. You are likely to tire of a theme design much faster than if you design a room that can easily be changed or updated by editing or adding one or two items.

Many of the rooms in this book are in homes around the world, and while it makes sense to have a Moroccan seating area in Tangiers, it can seem a bit awkward in a nineteenth-century American farmhouse. While it can be very fun and visually striking to create a room inspired entirely by one country—with fabrics, furniture, and carpets all from Indonesia, for example—you have to be careful not to limit yourself aesthetically. With theme rooms you are stuck in a particular look and are very limited in your choices. If you become bored with a design you will have to change the entire room. It is easier and less expensive to create rooms that are constantly evolving spaces that change according to your needs.

❖ ✳ ❖

TOP: *Use unusual global finds in new ways. Here, a bronze Thai rain drum makes a striking coffee table.*

BOTTOM: *Combine East and West. This classic Western-style sofa is perfectly framed by an Asian folding screen.*

DRESSING
THE FLOOR

anish bare floors and dress them up, instead, in brilliantly hued, beautifully patterned exotic rugs. From Peru to Tanzania there are antique or modern rugs to suit any home, from a beach bungalow in Mexico to a Manhattan penthouse. Many handmade rugs with their bold colors and sharp graphic designs are surprisingly contemporary and will instantly revive a tired room. But rugs are not just for floors, in fact for centuries rugs were treasured as valuable works of art that were too precious for the floor. Display rugs as wall hangings, tablecloths, and covers for chests and benches. Here are five favorite rugs from around the world.

Using Global Textiles

The living room is a wonderful and easy place to indulge in a passion for global textiles. Look at pillows, upholstery, tablecloths, curtains, throws, wall hangings, and lampshades as opportunities to experiment with exotic fabrics. Learn about fabric weights, textures, and materials to choose the best textiles for your needs. Let heavier fabrics, such as Kilims and Ewe cloth, upholster furniture. Place gauzy sheer fabrics, such as linen or cotton, on windows. Use more delicate pieces, embroidered or beaded fabrics, for example, as decorative pillows or even lampshades. Frame or hang antique remnants. Of course, every choice you make depends on how you will use your living space. If you have high traffic room with lots of children, you will want to choose sturdy, washable fabrics. If you want a space that is more of a showplace, indulge in more luxurious textiles.

You will find fabrics made for specific purposes such as curtains or upholstery on the market, but be creative if you don't find exactly what you need. If you come across fabrics in the right weight and size, you can use them to make your own items, from pillows to valances. When hunting for fabrics try textile districts, flea markets, and antique stores to find luxurious bolts, vintage upholstery, or antique remnants. Don't let awkward sizes and shapes frighten you away from a particularly spectacular textile. As many fabric aficionados will tell you, first find patterns and colors and materials that inspire you and then worry about what to do with them when you get home. Store textile collections folded and arranged by color or material in an open cabinet or shelf. When a specific project presents itself, from bolster pillows to curtains, you'll have a library of fabrics from which to choose.

LEFT: *Display global textiles predominantly throughout your living space as wall hangings, pillows, upholstery, and curtains. This living room celebrates the graphic designs and earthy shades of African fabrics.*

OPPOSITE: *When you find a showstopping textile with a fabulous combination of colors, repeat the color scheme throughout the room. The salmon, orange, and pink in the carpet of this Morrocan-style living area are reflected in the throw pillows, upholstery, and wall color.*

One way to incorporate dazzling exotic design into a room is to dress walls with gorgeous wallpapers inspired by global textures, palettes, patterns, and hues. Wall coverings have come a long way from predictable florals and stripes and are now available in a fantastic array of designs that truly celebrate international style. While paint can refresh a room, wallpaper can take it to new levels, completely transforming the space without changing a piece of furniture. Whether you prefer the lavish look of metallics, an aged patina, subtle texture, or an internationally influenced pattern, there are wallpapers for every room.

Try on Texture

Texture is the new pattern and there are a plethora of papers that showcase global materials. From bamboo, raffia, seaweed, and gold leaf Asian materials influence these wallcoverings. The look is warm, enveloping a room in the subtle details and intricacies of each texture's pattern. Earthy shades of browns and beiges recall the charm of a tropical retreat.

The Aged Look

For many seasoned collectors of antiques, the glossy look of a new piece of furniture or accessory is not appealing. Instead, the timeworn appearance of a treasure that has aged beautifully is what truly captures their attention. This fascination with patina has made its way to wallcoverings. Select papers that mimic the green patina of an exposed copper or a slightly tarnished silver or gold for a completely original look. A room dressed in these wallcoverings promises an eclectic and offbeat space.

Go Metallic

Opulent and dynamic, rooms covered in metallic papers get noticed. Since gold or silver is anything but understated, metallics often look better in smaller spaces such as a powder room, where the result will be confident but not garish. The latest designs are solid, textured, or patterned. These papers are inspired by a range of influences including the repeating gold squares of teapaper that line Chinese tea chests, embossed Chinese characters, and the alternating look of shiny and subdued geometries. Cover a room in a lustrous metallics for a space that is both luxurious and glamorous.

Play with Pattern

To enliven a room look for wall coverings embellished with glorious patterns, motifs, and symbols found from Malaysia to Morocco. These papers take their cue from patterns found in exotic flora and fauna, fabrics, art, and tile. For instance, designers have discovered that the graceful shape of a ginkgo leaf, the graphic shape of an African symbol, the swirling pattern of a mosaic tile floor, or the sumptuous design of a Indonesian textile provide ample inspiration for new designs. Color abounds, choose from pale pastels to strong zesty shades. The more pattern you have on the wall, the less you need in the room. Select solid hues and basic shapes to compliment a richly detailed wallpaper.

Organizing the Little Things

Stop searching for lost items! Instead, find a place for everything from paperclips to socks. Avoid those way-too-practical, ugly plastic storage bins or those lifeless plastic desk organizers. Instead choose exotic accessories that add some panache to a space as well as hold everything. Don't be limited by an object's intended purpose. Think creatively in terms of material, size, and shape to find storage solutions for an incredible range of items. Here's a round up of four global pieces that will have you organized in no time:

Buckets: Curved or square water buckets from China were traditionally used for transporting food and water. The thick wood planks and sturdy handle give the buckets their rustic appeal. They make a stylish container for magazines and newspapers next to a reading nook, or rolled towels in the bathroom.

Apothecary chests: If you are an adventurous decorator, try hunting down Chinese apothecary chests. Every chest has approximately thirty small drawers. Outside, circular brass rings and painted Chinese characters note the precise herb that would have been stored in specific drawers. The drawers are tiny but if you have lots of knickknacks (and a good memory) you can use them to store little odds and ends such as index cards, loose photos, office supplies, stockings, napkin rings, or extra candles.

Small covered boxes: Look for covered containers in a range of shapes, from circular Chinese spice boxes to triangular Chinese hatboxes. When you have an assortment of boxes, you will have just the right place for holding all those little extras that need a home such as paperclips, change, jewelry, or business cards.

Baskets: Basket weaving is an exquisite art form and you will find glorious global versions all over the world with some especially fantastic examples from Swaziland, the Philippines, and Indonesia. Baskets are crafted in a range of materials from rattan to bamboo. There are baskets in a dizzying array of shapes and sizes displaying every style from modern to rustic. Use baskets to store, arrange, and organize almost everything. Look for longer ones to store umbrellas or shallow ones for storing rolled tablecloths and napkins. Consider placing stationary in small, square woven trays or a few board games in larger versions. For multi-purpose pieces, covered baskets with sturdy flat lids make lovely tables.

OPPOSITE: *For stylish storage, nothing beats a gorgeous armoire and covered baskets as these Chinese versions illustrate. The sliding bamboo screen is a clever way to divide different areas in a small space.*

LEFT: *To keep the spotlight on vibrant colors, Indonesian art and sculpture—and not on clutter—bowls and boxes hold odds and ends from fruit to books.*

Exotic Sleeping Spaces

Your bedroom is the place where you dream, relax, and revive, so lavish your attention on making it a room that exudes a blissful sense of serenity. Fill your sleeping space with global items that delight your senses—incorporate sensuous textures, soothing colors, fragrant candles, world music, and cozy furniture. Whether you want your bedroom to be a minimalist retreat or a seductive hideaway, you can flirt with a variety of gorgeous international goods, from sheer Indian window panels for jazzing up your windows to antique embroidered Turkish pillows for punctuating your bed.

When designing your exotic bedroom, keep in mind that it's your own personal sanctuary, so it should be enhanced with items that are true expressions of your spirit. To personalize an exotic sleeping space, choose accessories and furniture that are bathed in your favorite hues, or reminders of travels past and future, or just treasures that you simply love. For example, try painting walls an intense color that you saw on a favorite trip—such as a rich Indigo inspired by Indonesia.

Don't just bring back pictures from your latest voyage; exhibit them in frames that you found on your journey—display photos from an Indian trek in, say, sari fabric frames. Collect art or sculpture that has a spiritual significance such as a treasured collection of Madonna-and-child paintings from Ecuador or happy Buddha statues from Myanmar. If you pull together items that you react to in a pos-

itive way emotionally—pillows in jaw-dropping colors, lanterns that send mosaics of light around your bedroom, or carpets in soft textures—you will have rooms that speak your visual language. The key is to personalize your bedroom so that is an inspired reflection of your spirit.

Global items in your bedroom will inspire dreams of adventures in far-off lands—a painted Moroccan octagonal table conjures images of nights in Marrakesh, or a bamboo-framed bed transports you to a balmy evening in Phuket. Exotic elements often serve as reminders of how many possibilities are outside your doorstep, and the bedroom is the perfect place to spark your imagination.

OPPOSITE: *Suspend mosquito netting from the ceiling over an all-white bed for a dreamy and romantic effect.*

BELOW: *A Moorish arched window and two Moroccan metal lanterns lend a romantic touch to a basic all-white bedroom.*

Furnishing the Bedroom with Exotic Treasures

Since most bedrooms are fairly small today, they don't demand a lot of furniture. You only need a wonderful bed or headboard along with soft bed linens, practical clothes' storage, roomy bedside tables, and, perhaps, comfy seating. Anything extra is up to you. The key here is comfort. Everything in your bedroom should be touchable and invite you to relax. If you find a cotton fabric with embroidered beading that looks fabulous but is scratchy, or a sexy divan that is uncomfortable, put those objects in other rooms where they can be looked at rather than touched. Here are a few ideas for functional and also alluring global furniture for the bedroom.

Headboards. Try covering a headboard with an unusual rich fabric such as a beautiful Thai silk or an antique floral Mexican altar cloth. Another chic option is to use a tall folding screen as a headboard. Look for Korean, Japanese, and Chinese screens that are painted with flora and fauna, daily life scenarios, or carved with geometric or scenic designs.

Bedside tables. Take a boring table and cover it in an exciting fabric such as a rich Javanese batik to a vibrant African Kente cloth from Ghana. Another fun idea is to find an attractive but sturdy table such as a mosaic topped wrought iron table from Morocco. Don't feel limited to using tables, try African or Chinese stools or Thai covered baskets. Just make sure you have enough room for a great read, a lamp, clock, and a water decanter.

Chests. Whether crafted for brides or voyages, brightly painted or beautifully carved, global chests are as practical as they are decorative. Depending on their size, chests can be used for more than just storage. They make roomy bedside tables, coffee tables, benches, or provide a sturdy anchor at the foot of a bed. Look for a range of looks from lacquered trunks with original hardware from China, brightly painted Mexican versions, or inlaid Syrian chests.

Baskets. There are some exquisite woven global baskets available from many countries with standout craftsmanship from the Philippines, Thailand, China, and Ecuador. Many designs were originally designed for carrying or storing food and grain. Look for baskets with sturdy lids that make a good side table, or an attractive laundry basket.

Scents. From potent to sweet global perfumes, incense, scented water, and candles provide new and exotic fragrances.

⁌ ✖ ⁍

LEFT: *For an arresting bedroom, hang a show-stopping fabric like this bold red-and-gold Indian tapestry in lieu of a headboard.*

OPPOSITE: *Place roomy and visually intriguing trunks such as this Moroccan marriage trunk at the foot of the bed to store extra bed linens and pillows.*

Creating a Serene Environment

All aspects of our lives have crept into today's bedrooms. Desks, televisions, computers, overflowing bookshelves, and cluttered vanities overwhelm bedrooms, making them living and working spaces instead of simply sleeping spaces. Eliminate this chaos in the bedroom by segregating the areas of your home for their specific tasks. The bedroom should be a sanctuary from the stress of the outside world. Make it a priority to design a bedroom that is a haven to quiet your mind after a busy day.

Consider banishing piles of bills, stacks of unfinished work, and flashing computer screens to another part of the house. If you do need to work in your bedroom, invest in functional and chic pieces that have plenty of storage such as an inlaid Syrian writing desk with several drawers for keeping files and papers. For a television, VCR, stereo equipment, or books, nineteenth-century and twentieth-century Chinese armoires are just the right size. Today, many armoires, even older versions, have been crafted to fit a TV. Look for armoires with additional nooks, drawers, and shelves to accommodate videos, folders, remotes

❖ ✳ ❖

TOP: *Make your bedroom a serene, uncluttered space by adding only a few simple decorative details such as this hanging Hindu lantern from India, ornate gilded and wood framed mirrors, a discrete armoire, and a rustic folding screen.*

BOTTOM: *To inspire dreams of far-off lands, incorporate exotic accents—such as this striking mosaic-framed mirror from Morocco—into sleeping areas.*

and other clutter. When you are finished watching television, close the armoire's doors and any mess that could be distracting will be hidden away behind a stylish facade.

Take a cue from upscale bedrooms in India that are simple in design but rich in color, detail, and textures. Many Indian boudoirs have a few stellar pieces of furniture such as an intricately carved teak bed and side tables, as well as vibrant textiles like hand-blocked cotton bedspreads, adorned with a few favorite objects such as traditional Hindu art and sculpture. The overall feeling in these bedrooms is serene.

he bed is the centerpiece of your bedroom, and since you spend one-third of your life sleeping, choose your bed wisely! The design of a bed sets the tone of a room, whether the style is casual, glamorous, or rustic. Most importantly, comfort is essential. If you are tossing and turning on a lumpy mattress or are kept awake by a creaky antique bed frame, it doesn't matter how fabulous your bed looks. Choose alluring bedroom furniture that is both comfortable and attractive. Whether you prefer sleeping on a mattress, futon, or Tatami mat, you will find a bevy of international beds from floor-level snoozing options to high canopy beds. Materials of global beds range from wrought iron, teak, bamboo, fabric, rattan, to decoratively painted wood. If you're looking for an ethnic bed that is totally original, here are a few of the more intriguing and unusual bedding concepts from around the world:

Lobi daybeds. Made by the Lobi tribe of Africa these wooden daybeds are smooth. They are slightly arched and sit low to the ground, measuring approximately 6 feet long and 3 feet wide. They are often taken outside and placed under a tree or in a family courtyard for an afternoon nap. These rustic daybeds can also be used as benches or as cocktail tables, or placed in front of a bed to store pillows and throws.

Futons. These Japanese beds are rolled up and stored out of sight in Tansu cabinets during the day. At night, futons are placed on Tatami mats directly on the floor for sleeping. In the West, futons are especially popular because they are inexpensive and often come with frames that can quickly convert into sofas. Futon mattresses provide firm back support.

Swing beds. Found in India and hung from the ceiling by metal chains that are often decorative, the swing bed holds a mattress suspended by a metal frame. The bed rocks slightly back and forth lulling you to sleep. For babies, swinging cribs are also popular. Smaller single beds are used as swings both indoors and on covered porches.

Hammocks. Believed to have originated in Central America, the hammock can be made from canvas, rope, or brightly decorated cotton. Always popular, there are hammocks on the market that are designed with frames or ones that are to be hung underneath a shady tree. Many people in hot climates, such as parts of Mexico and Brazil, prefer hammocks to beds.

K'ang beds. These centuries-old Chinese enclosed wooden beds were often used to keep warm during the winter. They would be used not just for sleeping but also as a living area a where family and friends would gather to talk.

Gurage headrest. A traveling bed of sorts, these small, hand-carved wooden blocks are from the Gurage tribe in Ethiopia. They have a deep arch to rest your head when you are ready to recline.

Bringing Exotic Textures and Patterns Home

*From Latin America to the Middle East, there are astoundingly beautiful ethnic patterns in textiles, furniture, tiles, carpets, and walls. From graphic to curvy, there are designs to suit your style. Artist and custom interior designer **Lucretia Moroni** is an expert at combining rich, intricate patterns from exotic lands. Here, she shares a few trade secrets on **how to combine global patterns**.*

Consider the number of colors in each pattern you use in a space. If you use many patterns from different global influences **stick to two or three colors**, or try using tone on tone jacquards.

When applying a pattern to a space think about its scale. Whether you are using pattern on walls, fabric, floors, or furniture **the scale has to match the proportion of the rooms**. The patterns you use shouldn't be too big or too overwhelming for a space.

Don't overdo it and cover walls, furniture, and floors with several different motifs. Choose one or two surfaces to display pattern, then keep other surfaces with textured colors, and borders to balance out the room.

Start with a room's architecture and add details and architectural elements to prompt an exotic room. Then choose the color scheme and patterns based on the proportion and scale of a space.

Lighting is the key to crafting an exotic space because it creates atmosphere. For window treatments, use linen gauze and other translucent materials in layers to help filter light and create a more exotic atmosphere.

Try mixing rich patterns in surprising ways. Experiment with pattern on modern furniture because it is an unusual look, and it goes against its own style.

You can **redesign a room** simply by adding borders, textured finishes, fabric, or wallpaper. Start by looking at the proportion of the room and the height and layout of furniture.

Creating an Exotic Bed

OPPOSITE: *Try using exotic fabrics in unexpected ways. The brilliant colors and intricate pattern of block-printed Indian textiles beautifully cover almost every surface, including the bedside table, bed, and wall.*

RIGHT: *For a graphic and modern look, punctuate the bedroom with earthy textiles in abstract patterns such as these potato-print fabrics from Zimbabwe. Design by Novika.com.*

As quickly as you can change the sheets you can transform a bedroom. Bedding, especially, determines the look and feel of the bed and also the room overall—muted neutrals inject a Zen feeling or the powerful pop of vivid Indian textiles add spice. A spirited mix of global textiles is an effortless way to incorporate color, pattern and pizzazz into your sleeping space. Sheets, pillowcases, throws, tapestries, bed skirts, curtains, and upholstery all combine to define the mood of a room whether it is sultry or sassy.

When you are selecting global bed linens, consider starting with basic cotton sheets for comfort and then layering exotic fabrics for bedcovers, decorative pillows, or on top of canopy beds. For a beautiful and simple bed, use white sheets—and let pillows, duvets, and bedcovers provide a burst of color, texture, or pattern. Try Chinese embroidered bedcovers made of silk that come in sexy hues and work perfectly on queen-size beds or just fit king-size beds. The Chinese covers' details and pretty designs also make wonderful wall hangings for the bedroom.

For another global alternative, saris or batik sarongs are the right size for flat sheets to fit twin beds or provide a pop of color when folded at the bottom of the bed. Indian bedcovers are very popular at the moment. Collectors love the luxurious decorative details and intense hues, including vibrant mirror inlaid fabrics, or arresting bed-

covers woven with Lurex threads. While there are many options for queen, full and twin beds, it is a little more of a challenge to find king-size global bed linens.

If you don't find the right exotic bed linens, make your own from beautiful fabrics. Duvet covers, shams, bed skirts, and pillowcases are easy to craft. If you don't have enough fabric for an entire duvet or pillow, use two different patterns, one for each side. If you have very small pieces or remnants, sew borders onto plain duvets or sheets to jazz them up. Look for fabrics that are soft and alluring like cottons, linens, velvets, and silks. If you find a stunning fabric that is delicate, you can still use it to dress the bed, just remove it for sleeping.

Dining Spaces

ABOVE: *Bring the outdoors in with abundant potted plants, plenty of light, and chairs made of natural materials.*

OPPOSITE: *Sophisticated exotic elements such as a Japanese-inspired lantern and a Tansu chest pair perfectly with modern cab chairs, elegant silver, and a traditional table.*

Whether your dining space is simply for entertaining or for everyday enjoyment, there are spectacular exotic elements to bring a dash of global style to your table. On the market you'll find everything that you need to add some spice to your dining space, from handcrafted tables such as Moroccan mosaic-topped versions to lively serving pieces like hand-carved Kenyan salad servers. For a table that celebrates multicultural design, mix in a few exotic elements with your own pieces—such as pairing luxurious French china with laminated chopsticks or Moroccan tea glasses with Ironstone plates.

Decide what mood you want your dining space to set. Do you want an Asian-inspired, low-level dining space with a low table and floor cushions, or would you prefer a more traditional Western table and chairs? Do you want a sophisticated room that is only used for dinner parties or do you want a more relaxed space for lively family gatherings each night? The level and formality of your dining area should be determined before you make your selections. Look for tables and chairs that accommodate your needs, whether you want a roomy table for large groups or a casual table that is unfussy and low-maintenance.

If you don't want to change your whole dining room, but you do wish to bring it from boring to brilliant, your best investments would be in buying a few stunning tablecloths, reupholstering chairs in ethnic fabrics, or adding exotic lighting. Whether you are using a lively batik from Indonesia or a pretty patterned jacquard, transforming the look of the dining room is as simple as changing the tablecloth.

For touches of global chic, try upholstering chairs in ethnic fabrics, such a luxurious Nigerian Asoke cloth embroidered with metallic threads or a colorful checkered cotton from Guatemala. Any chair, from a Louis XVI–style armchair to a midcentury modern version is given a new life by upholstering it in an exotic pattern or fabric that contrasts with its style. For example, try a bold, graphic pattern on an antique chair or a floral motif on a contemporary chair. Another easy idea that sets an exotic mood is to replace a boring light with a showstopping global light fixture such as a red Chinese silk lantern or an open metalwork star shaped chandelier from Morocco.

ABOVE: *In the Middle Ages, carpets were used to cover
tables because they were considered works of art too delicate to be stepped on. Let interesting and colorful rugs
dress the table. If they are not the right size layer the
carpet over a standard cotton or linen tablecloth.*

Bathing Spaces

Relax and unwind in global bathing spaces that are both functional and expressive retreats. Since you use your bathroom every day, utilizing everything daily from towels to tubs, make sure the bathroom is not only an efficient space but also one that promotes a sense of calm while you get ready for a busy day or recover after a hectic one. A common mistake is overlooking bathroom decor. A room you use so often for pampering and refreshing should be treated with the same respect as other larger spaces in the house.

Bring luxurious materials, furniture, and decorative accessories from around the world to make your bathing spaces true havens. Let global tiles, decorative mirrors, stools, baskets, screens, and carpets add personality to the bathroom. Of course, you need to select water-resistant materials for the bath, but you do have a world of options.

TOP: *Enjoy luscious fabrics and ornate furniture in the bathroom too. Use armoires for storing towels and toiletries, decorative screens for privacy, and rich textiles and carpets for color and pattern.*

BOTTOM: *To update a basic bathroom with upscale global style, add beautiful bamboo furniture and accessories and a real or watercolor rendering of an exotic flower such as an orchid.*

OPPOSITE: *Decorative handcrafted mirrors and tables along with textured walls set a Moroccan mood in Marrakesh.*

Bringing the World into Your Bathing Space

In a space that is normally quite small, adding one or two intriguing design elements will have maximum impact. To keep your bathing space fresh and original, keep fixtures white but add color, texture, and pattern with accessories. Here are a few ideas for bringing exotic elegance into your bathroom:

ABOVE: *To design a distinctive bathing space, try adding an unusual touch such as this unique copper-and-stone sink paired with hand-painted global tiles.*

OPPOSITE: *Replace boring white or solid-colored tile with vibrantly patterned, hand-painted tiles for a pretty bathing space.*

Mirrors. Take that boring medicine chest off the wall and, instead, place a global mirror above the sink. For an ornate look try a decoratively carved cedar mirror with floral motifs from Peru or place a more contemporary Mexican tin and Talavera tile mirror.

Armoires and cabinets. Look for armoires and cabinets, large or small to keep all your bathroom paraphernalia such as towels, toiletries, and cleaning equipment out of sight. Try decoratively painted Indian versions or relatively inexpensive bamboo cabinets.

Lighting. Banish unflattering fluorescent lighting from the bathroom and, instead, look for global lanterns, sconces, lamps, and candles.

Artwork. If you have empty wall space, add some color and pattern by hanging a global textile, painting, or watercolor. Try hanging interesting artwork or framing pieces of fabric. Just make sure you pick artwork that won't be damaged by the steam from a shower.

Seating. If you don't have a lot of space in the bathroom, look for small, wooden stools that can easily accommodate a stack of towels, books, or you. For larger bathrooms, bring in comfortable upholstered chairs covered in a global textile such as African Ewe cloth or a Kilim.

Baskets. Let covered baskets provide a space for laundry. Open baskets are a pretty way to hold rolled towels, makeup, and toiletries.

Textiles. Whether you like Indonesian batiks or Guatemalan tapestries, make your own window treatments and shower curtains from fabulous global textiles. In lieu of a standard shower curtain use an ethnic textile—make sure to create holes at the top of the fabric to line with a plastic shower liner. For an understated global touch, sew borders of exotic fabrics around the bottom of solid towels.

Major Changes

Retiling or remodeling a bathroom is a major undertaking, but can completely transform a dull bathroom into an exotic space that could be anywhere in the world. Look for brightly colored hand-painted tiles from Italy, Mexico, or Brazil. For a more subtle touch, try adding patterned border tiles to a room done in solid-colored tile. For something truly amazing, have a mosaic-tiled floor. Nothing is quite so jaw dropping as a solid-colored bathroom with a colorful graphic mosaic-tiled floor.

Another idea is to completely change the architecture of a bathroom. Create a Zenlike feeling with the linear aesthetic of a square tub, clean lines, and the neutral tones of stone tiles. For a Mediterranean look, use stucco walls painted bright white with brilliantly patterned tiles underfoot. Paint and paint treatments also lend an exotic feeling to a space, whether you are choosing a Chinese red for the bathroom or washing the walls in a rustic terracotta hue. Paint is probably the easiest and most inexpensive way to dramatically transform a room.

※

OPPOSITE: *Let this over-the-top traditional Moroccan bathing bathroom with a skylight and a circular stone tub inspire you to create unique spaces.*

Outdoor Spaces

Delight in the outdoors by creating exotic spaces that are as rich in color and textures as your favorite indoor rooms. Ditch those unexciting plastic loungers and tables that inevitably break and invest in beautiful sturdy global pieces that exude personality. Determine how you want to use your outdoor space and find global goods to enhance your experience. If you want to set aside a romantic spot in the garden to look up at the stars, cozy up to a Costa Rican cotton hammock built for two. For alfresco breakfasts, try teak tables and benches with batik cushions. If you are host to many summertime soirees, Indonesian colored-paper lanterns always brighten up an evening's festivities. For afternoon barbecues, have plenty of teak folding stools from Java or West African ebony benches on hand for an extra guest or two.

In many tropical climates from Brazil to Bali, outdoor areas are used as often as indoor ones. Many hours are spent relaxing, feasting, and socializing in verandas, courtyards, porches, terraces, and gardens. Take your cues from these outdoor rooms, from the lively balconies of Goa to the subdued chic of a Thai poolside. Design airy, carefree outdoor spaces inspired by global design from bountiful gardens to mosaic courtyards.

Selecting Outdoor Furniture

In the garden, on the porch or poolside, the secret to designing beautiful out-door rooms is in making your design look effortless. Planning a care-free space that allows you to enjoy the outdoors includes knowing what to expect—whether it's bad weather or lots of visitors. There is nothing chic about fussy spaces that cause worry about furniture getting ruined by the rain or the precise arrangement of pillows. If you have an open, uncovered garden space that you'd like to furnish year round, you must find materials that stand up to the elements. However, if you have a covered porch or balcony where furniture won't get wet, you have more flexibility as to what materials that you can use, from vibrant Kilim carpets to silk shantung pillows. Don't be limited by conventions of what defines indoor or outdoor furniture. There is something delightful about an antique wrought-iron garden chair nestled in a living room, or a sensational Syrian inlaid table brought outside to revel in the summer sun.

When looking for exotic furniture, there are a few basic materials that you will come across again and again. One of the most durable is teak. It is an exotic hardwood that stands up to any kind of weather, is resistant to rotting, and can be left outside year round. While teak's color will fade to a soft gray, it requires no treatment to protect it, and some manufacturers are so confident in teak that they offer a seventy-five-year guarantee. There is an impressive array of teak products, including tables, benches, doormats, and lounge chairs with wheels. You must make sure, however, that you only buy teak that is responsibly grown in a country that requires ecological considerations, such as reharvesting. Otherwise, purchase only antique teak pieces.

For more decorative garden furniture, look for the curvaceous forms of wrought-iron chairs or filigree folding screens, with particularly intricate crafting from India and Morocco. Make sure your wrought- iron furniture is treated with rust stabilizers and paint to hold up against corroding and rust. Another option is bamboo and rattan, although these elements are better placed under cover since they don't stand up as well to water, and bamboo bleaches out under harsh sun. Bamboo has a timeless quality and is commonly used indoors as well. For a colorful option, try mosaic tile-top tables from Mexico and Morocco.

TOP: *Large and small tiles create an exotic courtyard with a shallow fountain.*

BOTTOM: *A covered outdoor room blurs the line between indoors and out with luxurious furniture, a Moroccan star table, a wrought-iron lantern, and silk pillows.*

OPPOSITE: *Employ architecture to dictate an exotic mood such as these Moorish arches and white painted stucco that is evocative of Greece and Morocco. A wrought-iron chair stands up beautifully to the elements.*

ART CENTER COLLEGE OF DESIGN LIBRARY

Designing an Outdoor Space

Whether you are in the country sitting by the pool or catching the view from a tiny city balcony, take the time to design a chic and fun outdoor space. The time we spend outdoors is about joy—lounging in the summer sun, sharing an outdoor buffet with friends, or taking some time to work on the garden. Make sure your outdoor spaces are well-designed, functional, and fabulous retreats. A variety of exotic pieces can be used to enhance your outdoor room. Here are a few ideas for sprucing up your outdoor spaces, even if you don't have much of a view.

※

OPPOSITE: *Make your outdoor space as comfortable and luxurious as your indoor spaces. This seating area crafted from an abundance of colorful global textiles including rugs, tapestries, cushions, and pillows.*

FOLLOWING PAGE: *Here, blue-and-white Chinese porcelain jars and planters, a Chinese parasol and block-printed tablecloth transform a brick paved pool area from ordinary to extraordinary*

At the pool. Even the most basic pool can use a little zing. If you love to lounge, try teak loungers with waterproof cushions. Another option is to scatter roomy cotton floor pillows around the pool for resting between morning and afternoon swims. If you want to make your own pillows, find a sturdy water-resistant ethnic fabric and fill it with waterproof foam inserts. For a more classic look, try blue-and-white porcelain stools or wrought iron garden chairs. When you want to sit in the shade, let a Chinese parasol keep you under cover.

On the balcony. Even if you have a little balcony in a high-rise building, you can make it a retreat. Since you have the benefit of a covered space, you have more flexibility in the materials you can choose. While you can make the balcony a multipurpose space, it may be easier to pick one activity and design around that. If you want to design a place for cozy breakfasts and calm dinners, pick a table and comfortable chairs. Wicker, rattan, wrought iron, tile, and bamboo all make good materials for balcony furniture. The balcony is also a good spot for exercise and meditation; place Tatami mats on the floor for yoga and stretching and low cushions and candles for meditation. If you want a place to recline and read the latest novel, try a wraparound sofa piled high with pillows in ethnic fabrics. The key to making a city balcony a relaxing outdoor retreat is to add plenty of plants and flowers. Whether you add tropical citrus trees, plant an herb garden, or have seasonal flower boxes, verdant touches make a world of difference.

In the garden. Let garden designs from around the world inspire your garden plan. While it may not be possible to plant the same plants and flowers as a garden in an entirely different climate than your own, you can be influenced by the overall design of a garden space. Traditional Chinese gardens are considered a serious art form and the garden is seen as an artistic recreation of nature and a retreat from a busy world. Circular entrances, lotus ponds, bamboo groves, lattice screens, and arched bridges are all elements found in traditional Chinese gardens. Japanese gardens are calm, minimalist escapes with waterfalls, stone pathways, mossy rocks, and evergreen shrubs. Let different elements from global gardens influence your choices in your own garden plan. Whatever your garden design, place benches, stools, and chairs in key points so that you can enjoy the space you have created.

the right lights can turn an ordinary evening in the garden into a magical event. From floating tea lights to pressed-tin lanterns little sparks of exotic lighting can illuminate a party or cast a romantic glow on a private dinner. Obviously, you should always consult a lighting professional to wire lanterns and be extra cautious when using candles. Here are a few favorite garden lights:

Glass lanterns. Set candlelit lanterns along garden walkways for enchanting lit pathways or atop tables for a glowing centerpiece. For showstopping mood lighting, hang lanterns from the ceiling with a low wattage bulb. Some of the most exquisite lanterns are made in Morocco of colored glass and metal. They come in a variety of shapes and sizes. Popular versions include hexagonal lanterns with domed tops and arresting star lanterns. For another striking hanging lantern, try hand-blown colored glass Hundi lanterns from India. The originals are quite expensive, but you should be able to find reproductions very easily.

Torches. For practical garden lighting, look for torches made of iron and glass. Some of the best are made in India and are a sophisticated alternative to fun Tiki torches. Create enchanting pathways or define an outdoor room with lit torches.

Paper lanterns. To cast a celebratory glow on a fete, try using colored paper or fire-retardant canvas collapsible lanterns. Look for beautiful versions made in Indonesia and India. Another party favorite are Chinese paper and mesh-painted lanterns, as well as simple Japanese paper lanterns. Lanterns range in style and color from bold red-and-gold round Chinese lanterns to minimalist square white rice paper versions from Japan.

Pillar candles. For a modern arrangement, try setting square pillar candles on square Capiz dishes from the Phillipines, or square earthenware dishes from Japan. Placing a straight line of three or more candles makes a unique centerpiece or table arrangement.

Tea lights. When traveling throughout India and Southeast Asia, you may spot marble bowls filled with water and floating tea lights and flowers. This is a pretty and easy arrangement to reproduce.

ABOVE: *Place global lanterns along garden pathways, or, for a striking centerpiece, set one on top of an outdoor table.*

Exotic Mixes

Buying beautiful furniture and fabrics is easy, but blending old pieces with new ones to form an eye-catching, seamless space can be a challenge. Ideally, you want to design harmonious arrangements of disparate objects, styles, centuries, and cultures. However, the leap from gathering an assortment of furniture and fabrics to putting it all together is sometimes daunting. How do you know what styles will complement each other? How do you combine exotic color and pattern? How do you design around awkward spaces? One way to navigate potential decorating pitfalls is to decide what style you want each room to express, and then follow the rules for each look. Whether you prefer modern, romantic, classic, or eclectic style, this section will show you how to make your spaces true illustrations of you and your love of the exotic. ¶ Design is all in the details. Each choice you make contributes to a room's ambiance. Understanding how colors, furniture, textures, and art can highlight your favorite look will help you know what to search for and what to stay away from. A range of looks and styles come from every far-flung corner of the globe, and at every price. The vast selection of objects to choose from is incredible, but without a good road map, it can easily seem overwhelming. However, if you plan your spaces according to the basic design principles of your own personal style, your rooms will not only highlight the best of global design, they will also be spaces you'll love coming home to.

OPPOSITE: *Use art to focus attention and create a serene space. Here, a well-edited selection of international art and furniture, including a Robert Mapplethorpe photograph and a seated Thai Buddha, offer a calm haven. Interior by Vicente Wolfe.*

Modern Export

An amazing selection of contemporary, and centuries-old global fabrics, furniture, and art can be mixed together to create a stunning modern space. Designing a contemporary room using handcrafted antiques and fabrics might seem like a contradiction. However, what we view today as modern isn't about new, but about pared-down. Modern spaces are sleek, uncluttered rooms that highlight the clean architectural silhouettes of furniture and follow the age-old adage less is more. Often people see Japanese interiors and are impressed with how current they appear, even though the basic design of a traditional Japanese house has not changed since the sixteenth century. The Japanese home's neutral palette, multipurpose rooms, minimal low-level furniture, few decorative objects, and plenty of hidden storage space is a good example of how a well-edited space appears contemporary.

RIGHT: *Here, contemporary ash furniture is upholstered with hand-woven cotton fabric from Senegal. The bold repetitive patterns on the side chair and stool add global flair to modern design. Design by Claire Beaumont.*

Modern Exotic Design Basics

SETTING THE STAGE   Many modern spaces begin with white walls and bare floors, which provide a blank canvas for clean-lined furniture, striking pieces of art, and an uncomplicated color palette.

FURNITURE   The modern room is all about simplicity. Look for furniture with little decorative detail and a distinct profile—a smooth, hand-carved African bench, or a centuries-old Chinese armchair with an impressive sculptural form.

COLOR   For a modern color palette the neutral all-white look always works. If you want to add color, stick to graphic color combinations or simply add punches here and there, such as chairs upholstered with bold hues of Thai silk.

TEXTILES   Stick to solid hues and use large blocks of color or prominent linear and graphic patterns. Many Southeast Asian and African fabrics are both colorful and graphic. Look for textiles with bold, geometric designs in abstract patterns for a fresh look.

ART   Spotlight global artwork by following the Japanese tradition of displaying only one or two objects at a time. Let your favorite pieces of contemporary art take center stage, such as an arresting South African sculpture or a graphic Japanese scroll painting.

ABOVE: *An otherwise traditional room can be made to feel modern with bold colors and strong, graphic patterns, as seen with this abstract green-and-yellow wall treatment.*

OPPOSITE: *For a modern look, focus on furniture. The clean lines of this daybed and Chinese table lend an understated air.*

White Hot Color

ABOVE: *In a house in Bali, bamboo chaises are dressed in inviting and plush white cushions to bring this tropical furniture up to date.*

The color white is fresh, uncomplicated, and has the ability to modernize a room. Crisp white walls draw your eye to a room's architecture and details—from the lines of furniture to the design details of accessories. In modern rooms that favor spare and well-chosen treasures, white walls act as a spotlight. Galleries and museums often utilize white walls to draw attention to the art.

Imagine a grouping of dazzling pieces from around the globe—Italian low-level sofas, a square lacquer Chinese table reinterpreted as a cocktail table, two smooth hand-carved African stools, a collection of Japanese pottery, and nine square, black frames with vintage Kente cloth remnants. Place all these elements in a room painted a light pastel, or perhaps covered in Indian chintz wallpaper, and the room takes on a romantic mood. But place the objects in a room bathed in white, and their linear forms and minimalist design take center stage— exuding a confident, contemporary exotic flavor.

White is a fountain of youth, a unifying element that pulls together modern and exotic riches. Upholstering furniture in white adds an immedi- ate update to any piece, whether it is a nineteenth-century daybed from Nepal or an Indonesian rattan side chair. Covering many older pieces in white provides an instant face-lift and contrasts boldly with tropical woods. When you design a white room, mix various shades, from cool to warm, as well as a range of textures, from linens to silks. Combine furniture from different centuries and cultures, unifying the various styles with a palette of whites on upholstery, accessories, walls, curtains, and pillows.

OPPOSITE: *In a Lon* *paired with a Chir* *dazzling visual st*

RIGHT: *Contrast w* *on grouping geom* *here with the Asia* *a Western bedroo*

Combining Modern Riches

ABOVE: *Choose modern furniture with a clean-lined, pared-down look and global pieces mesh perfectly—like this living space that combines modern ottomans and chaise, an African stool, and a Chinese table.*

OPPOSITE: *Mix styles and cultures for a sleek, contemporary room.*

Often, people design their spaces with familiar objects because they worry that global furniture and accessories won't work with their own pieces. Don't get stuck in the rut of only decorating with elements from one time period, one style, or one culture. For example, if you only use midcentury modern American furniture, everything will go together, but you are limiting yourself aesthetically. Mix in a handcrafted Brazilian table, Japanese paper lanterns, and some Nigerian George fabric curtains, and then you have a room that is a knockout.

The key is to look at objects the way a designer would. Select global pieces for their shapes, hues, and purpose, keeping in mind how they will complement your existing design. A west African stool carved from one piece of wood, an Eames lounge chair, and a Chinese cinnabar-red lacquered armoire can occupy the same space beautifully, but it helps to have a common thread when linking diverse patterns and forms. Color is one way to pull everything together—use touches of the same hue or repeat a color scheme throughout a room for a seamless look. Another way to link a variety of modern items is to concentrate on the geometry of your pieces—blend curvy with angular and linear with circular. Look for distinctive shapes and silhouettes that contrast and complement each other to create interest in a space.

Hunting and Gathering

If you are a collector, the thrill is in the hunt—uncovering that enchanting rare blue-and-white Chinese porcelain urn or a playful Indonesian shadow puppet. When you get home with whatever delights that you've picked up on travels or at the local antiques shop, your next challenge is to figure out how to organize and where to exhibit your goods. For a modern space this question becomes more difficult since the pared-down aesthetic of a contemporary dwelling doesn't call for lots of anything.

Displaying collections successfully calls for careful editing—nothing looks worse than a tabletop filled to the brim with a random assortment of items, each one having nothing to do with the other. To pack a visual punch using modern export treasures, make sure to link similar types of objects such as an assorted collection of Portuguese Capiz bowls in varying colors and sizes, or a grouping of Buddha sculptures from different countries. Your collection will be more visually powerful if you allot a tabletop, shelf, or wall as exhibition space and place a carefully arranged grouping in this one area.

If you have plenty of storage, another option is to rotate your displays. One month you could showcase a few copper batik caps and another month you could show off several Peruvian statues. Try to keep displays simple. For example, in a room with minimal furnishings you only want to showcase one or two collections. In a modern space a display should be an intriguing accent, one that invites conversation but doesn't overpower the room.

❖ ✳ ❖

TOP: *Employ color to play up or minimize awkward spaces. Here, a small, recessed area stands out when bathed in a strong red to contrast with the yellow of the rest of the room. Display collections of similar objects together, like these carved pre-Columbian figurines, to make the arrangement more powerful. Design by Lucretia Moroni.*

OPPOSITE: *To pack a visual punch, hang similar artwork in groups, like lining eight prints of Andy Warhol's Mao along one wall.*

Paring Down

For a room or house to evoke true, modern glamour, editing a space is just as important as adding to it. A modern room is visually intriguing because of the pared-down and perfected arrangement of objects, as well as the open uncluttered space that surrounds them. Clutter is a common problem as we are constantly amassing papers, objects, and knickknacks. In addition, with the Internet and frequent travel, it is incredibly easy to access many different cultures and their treasures. But the buy, buy, buy, mantra that pervades American culture doesn't work for a minimalist. So one of the most important steps in designing a modern space is to purge. Donate or sell items that you don't use, don't love, and don't need. Edit your rooms to clean your space of that random junk, tired accessories, and outdated fabrics. To highlight minimalist design, get rid of anything that is too busy or ornate. After editing your room, you want to be left with striking pieces with clean lines.

The next step is finding storage for everything you do need in your home. Houses that are lived in have a certain amount of clutter culprits, including toys, loose papers, magazines and newspapers, and pocket change. The key to creating a pared-down global space is finding a place for all the stuff of everyday life. Look for pieces that are appealing to the eye and still provide plenty of hidden storage. From India to South Africa, you will find exceptional chests, armoires, cabinets, and boxes that all do the trick of stylishly hiding away clutter. Don't use plastic bins or cardboard boxes; instead, look for striking items that you can display. Try showing off an antique Tibetan lacquered trunk for toys or a sleek, leather jewelry box from Ghana. After editing and finding a place for everything, not only will you be more organized, but the contemporary furniture, fabrics, and art in your home will take center stage.

Eliminate clutter and keep things simple to highlight global modern furniture. Design Tucker Robbins.

Romantic Export

Fall in love with exotic rooms that exude romance. Two decades ago, if you were to read an interior-design magazine about romantic design, more often than not you would see houses bathed in chintz, lace, and many shades of pink. Today, romantic rooms are much more than that tired cliché and global patterns and accessories form an ideal marriage with romantic style (in fact, chintz, which people think as traditionally English, actually originated in India).

Envision a sexy boudoir with a red Chinese canopy bed draped in a sheer mosquito netting and covered with red-and-yellow silk-embroidered bedcovers, or a living room with fabric covered walls, Moroccan lanterns, and vibrant Thai silk floor pillows. Handcrafted global furniture, textiles, and art with centuries of history behind their techniques and inspiration are perfect building blocks for constructing a room with a romantic vibe. Today, romantic rooms are alluring places infused with a seductive range of colors, punctuated by intriguing patterns, and bathed in sensuous textures that feel luxurious.

The romantic room doesn't hold back from astounding and delighting—so feel free to fearlessly combine intricately patterned fabrics and decoratively carved furniture. In fact, the romantic space will have you swooning over walls covered in Indian block-printed fabrics or star-shaped lanterns, which cast a glow through more than eighty panes of glass. There is no minimalism here, furniture is inlaid, elaborately carved or lovingly painted, and fabrics are brocaded, embroidered, beaded, fringed, and appliquéd. International accessories are a perfect match for a romantic style. The only trouble that you'll have is in restraining yourself from collecting all the unbelievably fantastic exotic design elements available to you.

❧ ✦ ❧

OPPOSITE: *Luxuriate in romantic spaces that thrive on powerful combinations of sumptuous color and pattern with fabric-covered walls, inlaid furniture, and beautifully detailed decorative accessories.*

TOP: *For a mosaic of pattern, cover almost every surface with different designs.*

BOTTOM: *Combine bright color and rich pattern. Here, the intricate patterns of mosaic-tiled walls surround brilliant shades of bright silk ottomans and pillows.*

to create a romantic mix, focus on design elements that transport and indulge all five senses. When decorating for the senses, always purchase items that you can see and touch rather than buy on the Web. You alone understand the powerful effect that objects have when you run your fingers along a marble sculpture or hear the sound of chandelier crystals. ¶ When examining global goods close up, you'll notice their remarkable craftsmanship and the subtle signs of wear that give a glimpse into an object's past. As you design your home, remember that you are not simply designing for visual effect; you are creating rooms that will be lived in and will be experienced by all five senses. To decorate a romantic room you must understand the importance of pampering and spoiling your senses with gorgeous objects, enchanting sounds, intoxicating scents, sensuous materials, and delectable treats. Here are a few ideas to get you started:

Sight. Patterned surfaces, jaw-dropping color, dazzling artwork, and artful arrangements all delight the eye. Choose hues, shapes, and art that inspire you. Don't be afraid to cover surfaces in pattern and bright color. The key is to trust your instincts. A few different patterns can be used in one space, but try and link them in some way whether it be the type of fabric, country of origin, or a common color palette. A color wheel is a good way to learn how various shades can be combined effectively. Another good design tool (and trick of many interior designers) to help you see how everything will look together is to make bulletin board with fabric samples and paint chips for every room you decorate. Another key element is lighting to set a romantic mood. Let assorted candles, lanterns, and colorful fabric covered lampshades create a soft glow.

Sound. Playing world music is a wonderful way to add an exotic feeling to a space. Go to a local music store and explore the world music section. Get a feel for what music you like from the sultry rhythms of a Cuban salsa band to the soft crooning of an Arabic pop star. World music is a refreshing break from the most popular and often-overplayed hits. Don't worry if you can't understand the words, it's all about rhythm. Another option is to introduce a small fountain or wind chimes for a calm Zenlike infusion of sound.

Touch. From sexy, soft velvets to the cool feel of Mexican tiles underfoot alluring materials are essential to a romantic space. Anything that

looks good but doesn't feel good should be edited out. Add texture underfoot with flat-weave rugs, coir mats, or mosaic tile. Make chairs, beds, and sofas inviting with rich fabrics including velvets, silks, damask, kente cloth, ikats, batiks, or brocade.

Smell. Fill your space with bold and subtle scents that remind you of such places as the banks of the Nile, beaches in Brazil, or the bazaars in Istanbul. Scent is a powerful force that can stir memories and create new ones. Gather perfumes, scented oils, candles, and flowers from far-off destinations to evoke the spirit of other those places. Collect various fragrances, from the strong scent of Indian incense, or the delicate fragrance of fresh Lotus flowers, to the sexy smell of jasmine candles.

Taste. Chances are you are familiar with world foods from spicy Indian dishes to healthy Japanese sushi. However, there are always new flavors and recipes to sample from leeche fruit from Southeast Asia to Ecuadorian ceviche. Treat yourself to a new cuisine every week by trying a new restaurant or following recipes from an ethnic-foods cookbook. Another trend to try is fusion cuisine, which blends flavors, ingredients, and spices from two or more regions.

ABOVE: *Brightly pattened pillows provide a burst of pattern in a simple and pretty bedroom.*

OPPOSITE: *Bowls with floating candles and fresh fragrant flowers are commonly seen throughout Southeast Asia and India. They make sexy, sweet-smelling centerpieces.*

Creating a Romantic Mood

Express a romantic mood in any room by adding just the right exotic touches—use the power of color, decorative details, and soft lighting to create ambiance. Again, details make all the difference, such as lining a garden walkway with candles or enveloping a canopy bed in a gauzy silk. Romantic rooms are not about being practical. They are instead about the power of design to transform a space and enchant those who enter it.

Display objects to show off the beauty of their silhouette and their lovely details. Hang an interesting grouping of African carved masks that express a range of moods, or exhibit one amazing Nepalese sculpture prominently. Fill romantic spaces with pieces that hold personal significance, whether you acquired them on a special trip or because they simply make you smile. Spotlight photos of your friends and family in handcrafted global frames, made from such beautiful materials as Mexican silver or Filipino mother-of-pearl. Consider hanging painted landscapes of places you've visited (or hope to), or place glorious travel books on tables

TOP: *Hammocks always evoke a carefree glamour that invites you to relax.*

BOTTOM: *An inspiring mix of silks and sheer netting turn this canopy bed into a retreat from a busy day.*

OPPOSITE: *Surround yourself with colors you love by covering walls and beds in that hue or simply adding small bursts here and there.*

to inspire your journeys. Let stunning fabrics shine by placing them all around the room. Try draping a Chinese fringed silk shawl over a chair, or toss a sheer gold Thai scarf over a lamp, or cover a headboard in a tapestry weave fabric from the Philippines. Realize that every little detail can enhance a gorgeous global room.

Color is a key element in creating a romantic design. Select hues that you respond to and cover walls, ceiling, beds, curtains, and sofas with shades of that color, balancing it out with complementary tones. Other countries such as India use color much more freely and it seems that every corner of that country is pulsating with alluring hues. Legendary *Vogue* editor Diana Vreeland once noted that pink was the navy blue of India. Let India's fearless use of strong and dazzling color inspire your own palettes and say goodbye to safe beiges and creams.

Be bold with color. If you have a passion for purple or you find that pale blue calms you, surround yourself with those shades. Romantic rooms use color to energize, soothe, or enchant.

Next, create arrangements throughout the house that are purely for your enjoyment. If you are a writer, craft a cozy writing nook next to a window piled high with floor cushions from Thailand and throws from Italy. If you are an avid cook create a kitchen that celebrates your passion with bowls, dishes, and glasses from all over the world. Romantic spaces are expressions of what you adore, whether it is a hobby or a favorite color.

An easy way to set a romantic vibe in any room is with lighting. Think candles, lanterns, chandeliers, and sconces that let light flicker and dance around a space. Lanterns of colored and clear glass or cutout designs in pressed tin allow light to create patterns on the walls. If you love candles look for unique candleholders such as Tunisian glass teacups or circular, mosaic candleholders from Brazil.

❧ ✺ ❧

OPPOSITE: *Inviting daybeds are made even more welcoming with a large throw and comfortable cushions.*

TOP: *Often used in the tropics mosquito netting does more than just keep bugs away—it sets a romantic tone. Here, mosquito netting is hung with tabs along a four-poster bed.*

BOTTOM: *Torans from India make unique and colorful valances.*

Classic Export

If you're a fan of classically chic rooms, you appreciate designs that never go out of fashion. Sometimes, rooms decorated in a more traditional style need global export treasures to bring them to life. A common misconception is that unless you have an adventurous or bohemian sense of style, exotic items are not for you. Another fallacy is that those with more conservative tastes who love the charm of antiques should only decorate with such enduring styles as French, American, and English antiques. This is absolutely not the case, as the rooms in this chapter illustrate. In fact, spaces that are only decorated with traditional antiques often look dated and dull.

To keep classic rooms looking fresh and fabulous, use little touches of global style for intriguing results—you'll find that an unexpected object or two keeps design spontaneous. No matter what your style is, you can find international pieces that are reflections of your aesthetic interests, whether you are an absolute classicist or in love with bohemian chic.

If classic is your style, look for pieces that are more traditional in their shapes and design such as a Colonial-style teak and rattan bed or the always in vogue blue and white porcelains of China. Stay away from trendy or flashy looks, and stick with export items that are timeless. Always in style combinations of subdued color palettes, familiar forms, and traditional furniture arrangements are the calling card of classic style.

OPPOSITE: *A serendipitous match, an ornate Chinese altar table fits perfectly as a mantel.*

BELOW: *Unified by an understated palette of cream, French armchairs, antique ceramic pots, a reclining armchair from India, and a Chinese armoire evoke a classically elegant mood.*

ABOVE: *Choose items with simple lines and understated elegance for a timeless look. Here, an international blend of objects including a sisal rug, hand-carved Chinese and Moroccan tables, blue-and-white Chinese porcelain, and overstuffed, contemporary white sofas were chosen for their classic style.*

Timeless Export

Chinoiserie, safari-style, and Colonial-style furniture, like the little black dress, never go out of vogue. These looks are a wonderful way for a classicist to enjoy furniture with global inspirations. While these styles gained popularity centuries or decades ago, they now appear so often in Western interiors that we hardly think of them as exotic.

In the early part of the twentieth century, when well-heeled men and women went to Africa on safari, mosquito netting and animal prints surged in popularity. Today, there are many adorable faux animal skin and jungle print, picture frames, rugs, jewelry boxes and upholstery to add a dash of safari chic to your place. Try upholstering a chair in leopard-print fabric or tossing a zebra print throw onto an all-white bed.

Each colony's local craftsmen see the British influence upon furniture in their colonies, including India and parts of South America, in handmade Colonial furniture. The pieces inspired by European styles utilized local materials such as teak, rattan, Shesham wood, and cane. Colonial-style pieces are classic in shape and style but bear the stylistic renderings of the craftsperson and the country's own stamp.

TOP: *Celebrate safari style with colonial furniture such as this rustic bed from Bali.*

BOTTOM: *For a sophisticated look, decorate with antique Chinoiserie pieces, such as this red Chinoiserie secretary.*

For centuries, Western civilization has been fascinated by Eastern design. In the seventeenth century, as trade increased with China and Japan, Westerners' interest in the Orient reached new heights. Luxurious porcelains, textiles, fans, and furniture from Asia captivated Europe with their unique motifs, extravagant decoration, and impressive craftsmanship. Oriental items were especially popular with European upper classes and royalty, who could afford the steep prices these goods commanded.

However, the supply often did not meet the incredible demand, and Asian treasures were expensive and out of reach for most. Capitalizing on the trend, European artisans began reproducing and reinterpreting the ornate and fanciful motifs of human figures, architecture, and exotic birds and flowers that they saw on the imports onto European furniture. Classic pieces such as armoires, secretaries, and settees were adorned with Asian motifs, resulting in chinoiserie, a sophisticated style still in vogue today.

ABOVE: *Achieve sleek sophistication with a well-chosen Asian-inspired piece.*

OPPOSITE: *It's all in the details. This George I–style bureau bookcase is both exotic and classic.*

By the eighteenth century there was no area of the arts that hadn't been influenced by chinoiserie, including architecture, tapestries, furniture, ceramics, metalwork, textiles, and garden design. Even the paintings of French artists Jean-Antoine Watteau and Francois Boucher were inspired by Oriental art. European artisans were clever in imitating what they could not reproduce exactly, from copying Chinese blue-and-white porcelain to creating the look of lacquer. While the rage for chinoiserie waned in the nineteenth century, the 1930s revived the style, and the lively designs are still being reproduced today. If you'd like to add classic and upscale design to your space, incorporate a few pieces into your decor. From chinoiserie accessories, such as trays and boxes, to furniture, such as an exquisite replica of an eighteenth-century secretary, there is a range of beautiful chinoiserie items currently available.

Texture

For added depth in a room, use new and antique global pieces in a spirited assortment of materials and surfaces. Seasoned collectors of antiques and vintage pieces know that the original patina, even if it is fading, or slightly cracked, or the paint is peeling, is part of the charm of an older piece. Look for the crackled glaze of a Celadon jar or a three-panel screen with faded painted figures or the detailed worn surface of a hand-carved Indian door.

Classic rooms benefit from using unexpected textures and fabrics, especially when they are applied to traditional shapes and forms. For example, upholster a basic club chair in beige, Turkish linen, cover it with a red, paisley patterned shawl from Kashmir, and add pillows fashioned from red Chinese brocade? The look is still traditional, but the materials are global and introduce several textures. Rooms that stay within one color palette, creams and whites for example, especially benefit from

combining objects with varying textures. If you designed a room entirely upholstered in white cotton with mahogany tables and chairs, the space would be predictably, a huge yawn. But replace those dull pieces with furniture and accessories made of wrought iron, solid wood, rattan, and stone, as well as fabrics in silks, cotton damask, and linen, adding a touch of color to the walls, and woven carpets on the floor, and that same room comes alive.

Differing textures are not only interesting in terms of touch, but they keep a room visually rich. If you have a lot of one type of surface, add a material with an opposite texture. Try combining the roughness of a coir carpet with a soft velvet upholstered sofa. Pair a smooth marble sculpture from Burma with a grouping of hand-woven African baskets, or hang a vintage appliquéd fabric against a wallpapered backdrop. Be creative and use varying textures in every space that you design.

Classic Global throughout the House

The classic global room is one that perfectly combines traditional Western pieces with subtle and sophisticated touches of exotic elements. Try replacing basic items such as chairs, beds, curtains, lamps, rugs, and art with handcrafted international objects. Classic rooms all have a few things in common—they are understated in their design and reference the past as well as the present. Unlike romantic spaces that often need lots of color or pattern, a classic global space sometimes simply benefits from one or two minor changes. These updates can be very inexpensive accessories or antiques that are long-term investments. One replacement in each room can turn a bland space into an exotic interior. Here are a few easy and quick changes.

Living rooms. A common seating arrangement in Western living rooms is a sofa, two chairs, and a cocktail table. Try replacing one of those Western elements with an exotic piece to fashion a classic global living space. A good example is a white upholstered sofa and an eighteenth-century English mahogany cocktail table flanked by two nineteenth-century Chinese horseshoe chairs—the look is incredibly sophisticated and takes advantage of Chinese as well as English antiques. Another option is to cover bland throw pillows in a colorful textile such as mirror-inlayed fabric from India or earth-toned Kuba cloth.

Bedrooms. Colonial four-poster beds crafted in India or rattan and wood sleigh beds made in Indonesia are a good way to bring classic style to the bedroom. Consider using Thai raw silk for curtains in solid colors or sewing a border of a patterned global fabric on the bottom of plain white curtains. On a classic bed try an Indian embroidered bedspread or simply add one small boudoir pillow upholstered in a luxurious international fabric.

Bathrooms. Rather than sticking with white or solid-color tiles try incorporating border tiles from Italy or Mexico, or even designing a graphic mosaic tile floor. Another option is to place a hanging lantern from Morocco or Mexico suspended from the ceiling. Use covered and open woven baskets in varying sizes for holding jewelry, soaps, toiletries, rolled towels, and laundry.

Dining spaces. Mix in Thai celadon pieces with your own china. Upholster or slipcover dining chairs and cover tables in global fabrics. Use chopsticks instead of silverware. Look for bamboo-handled flatware or bamboo and rattan placemats. Serve tea in Japanese teapots or covered Asian teacups.

Home offices. Organization and a few interesting accessories are the key to a stylish home office. Look for lamps crafted interesting bases such as Japanese porcelain jars or African woven baskets to add some understated global sophistication to your desk. Another simple touch is to incorporate interesting textiles such as resist-print fabrics from Southeast Asia or brightly colored cottons from Central America to cover a bulletin board or upholster an office chair. Look for lacquered boxes from Japan or woven straw Filipino boxes for storage.

ABOVE: *In the living room a seventeenth-century Chinese Coromandel screen has been fashioned into an armoire and fits in with Regency style chairs and a Heppelwhite card table.*

BELOW: *The decorative detail in this dazzling nineteenth-century Indo-Portuguese spool bed is highlighted by white bed linens and understated furnishings.*

Eclectic Export

Eclectic rooms are exciting knock-your-socks-off spaces that break all the rules. With no color wheels or diagramed approaches to decorating, these rooms are unique reflections of their owners' varied and sometimes unruly taste. Eclectic spaces thrive on unexpected use of color and pattern, surprising juxtapositions and complete redefining of an object's purpose. Those with eclectic style don't want to be limited by preconceived notions about how rooms, houses, and gardens are supposed to look and feel.

Let eclectic rooms inspire you to indulge your original brand of style. Don't be confined by labels, instead, feel free to make your own choices based on your own interests, passions, and lifestyle. Instead of browsing at a flea market and not picking up those African masks you've had your eye on because you worry that they won't go with anything you have, bring them home and know that you will find a place for them. After all, everything you choose is a reflection of you. If you are drawn to an object or pattern, you can make it fit among other pieces of furniture and art that you have also chosen with the same gut instinct. Admittedly, this is sometimes difficult to pull off—there is something comforting about knowing that if you follow certain rules rooms will fit in terms of scale and mixes. But if you've already mastered the basics of design, trust in your power to create a unique space. Eclectic rooms sometimes require a certain amount of aesthetic trial and error, but that is how every artist and designer discovers his or her own look.

⊰ ❈ ⊱

ABOVE: *Instead of placing the expected candlesticks or picture frames on a mantle, try combining a medley of global sculptures and art.*

OPPOSITE: *For maximum impact, arrange an assortment of treasured objects. Here, African sculpture and contemporary art form a striking arrangement.*

Juxtaposition

Part of the appeal of a global eclectic space is in the unusual but often fabulous results that come from juxtaposing different looks. The fun comes from the whimsical mixing and matching of entirely disparate elements. Try blending items that you never thought would look good together. You will find that they play off each other perfectly. In exotic rooms that showcase designs from around the world, this union of objects that have nothing in common happens without any effort. Having the world be your marketplace to pick out the most astounding and alluring fabrics, furniture, and art opens entirely new worlds and fresh opportunities for design.

Experiment with new looks, such as hanging hand-painted cotton curtains from Indonesia on a traditional brass-ring curtain rod. Try blending antique with contemporary, such as upholstering a wingback armchair with a Nigerian Asoke fabric. Display art and sculpture that appeals to you on a completely visceral level such as Tibetan bronze statues next to hammered copper vases from Nepal alongside a decoratively painted Mexican copper plate. Showcase rustic paintings in upscale frames or exhibit international landscapes in a loft apartment. Use a carved Indian door as the front door of a Georgian townhouse. There is power in combining unexpected items, so freely pair refined with rustic or old with new or graphic with traditional. If your first instinct is that one color calls out for another or a piece of furniture looks like it would need a certain type of upholstery, go in the opposite direction and try something entirely new. Enjoy the visual surprise that comes from juxtaposing global treasures.

Breaking the Rules with Color and Pattern

When traveling through India, the first thing you notice is that almost every surface seems bathed in dazzling colors. In India there is a respect for the powerful effect of vibrant colors to enliven a room or make a woman appear more beautiful. Be inspired by global use of color and the fact that the Western conventions of color simply don't apply in other parts of the world. In the West it is common to stick with neutral beige tones or the timeless pairing of blue and white in an interior because color seems too difficult to master. Eclectic rooms are bold adventures in color and in use of global patterns, fabrics, and colors.

To break the rules with color, you don't need to paint a room ten different colors or purposely pair clashing hues, but don't be afraid to if it works for the space. If you study global fabrics, Indian sari fabrics or African Kente cloth for example you will be exposed to entirely new palettes such as pairing pink with red or combining yellow, black and green. If you love the way unusual color combinations look in ethnic textiles, try repeating those combinations in a room's overall palette.

Eclectic spaces fearlessly mix opposing patterns such as geometric with floral or circular with angular. Find inspiration in exotic textiles, furniture, carpets, and artwork—study how other artists and designers successfully combine motifs. If you are

interested in mixing patterns, observe Moroccan mosaic tile design, or the enlivened use of pattern in a painted Punjabi cabinet, or the incredibly intricate detail of a Tibetan carpet. Certain designs that seem completely carefree and spontaneous are the result of an artisan's years of careful study. The same is true for the best eclectic rooms—they are the result of the careful study of the principles of design and illustrate an original, bold, and visionary direction.

ABOVE: *A zany mix of colors and patterns this kitchen takes advantage of open cabinets.*

OPPOSITE: *Mix large-scale bold patterns with delicate ones for a unique look.*

Odd Spaces

Most houses have rooms that are awkward or imperfect in some way, such as low ceilings, oddly shaped areas, or lack of natural light. Eclectic rooms flirt with those little flaws, sometimes hiding them, other times playing them up. In eclectic exotic rooms, let quirky global pieces take center stage, distracting the eye from a room's imperfections. In a small, dark room, make the space a standout by stenciling dazzling geometric motifs on the walls. Repeat a favorite motif along each wall—an interesting symbol from Zimbabwe, perhaps, or a pattern derived from a mosaic tile design. If a room doesn't get a lot of light—bathe it in vibrant color and keep the furnishings light. In an awkward empty alcove, create a low-level seating area or children's play space with Tatami mats, or add a daybed or table that fits the space perfectly. Turn a small space into a tearoom with floor cushions and display an array of global teapots around the room. Transform the attic into a meditation room, creating a sanctuary to quiet your mind with a small fountain, a floor pillow, and candles. Be creative about lack of storage space—instead, seize the opportunity to create an interesting display of your treasures. Don't ever look at a challenging space and think that it is hopeless, instead, have fun with it and see an opportunity to create a unique design.

ABOVE: *Chinese characters become graphic designs when repeated on wallpaper.*

OPPOSITE: *Make the most of awkward spaces. Here, an alcove is turned into a cozy haven with a daybed.*

Old Things, New Ways

One of the most exciting aspects of interior design is creating completely personal spaces designed to enhance your day-to-day life. You can achieve this by decorating around your lifestyle, interests, and personal taste. Every aspect of your rooms, from the rugs to the lighting, should be carefully selected to work for you. The key to putting it all together is to see the possibilities in every object. When you are shopping for global design elements, look at every piece with fresh eyes. Don't worry about what the intended purpose is—simply figure out if an object can be transformed into what you need. For instance, a bamboo brush pot can be used as a vase in the dining room, a pencil-cup in your office, or cooking utensil holder in the kitchen.

Look at the material, texture, shape, and size to determine how a new global piece would suit your design. For instance, a tall wooden storage vessel from India makes a rustic umbrella stand or a home for rolled blueprints. One brightly painted, low-to-the-ground Punjabi chair makes a perfect children's chair, a fun place to hold books, or a relaxed perch for enjoying the garden. Eclectic rooms often highlight objects in unexpected ways: take a brightly colored beaded Yoruba chair from Nigeria and use it at the head of a dining table, or look for interesting Mexican pottery or Burmese sculpture and have them made into lamp bases. Punctuate your rooms with visual surprises: in a classically designed house line a traditional mantle piece with wood sculpted figurines from West Africa or cover 1950s modern bar stools in Kuba cloth or a woven Ikat. Have fun when you design a space—design should be both innovative and playful.

CREDITS

Courtesy of Amdega Ltd., 84 (left)

Tim Street-Porter/beateworks.com, 14; 24; 72; 86 (top); 103; 110; 116; 117 (bottom)

Courtesy of Burton-Ching, 122; 123

Frick Byers, 17

Christopher Coleman Design/Pieter Estersohn, photographer, 131

Claire Dishman, 18; 97

Fernando Bengoechea/Franca Speranza, srl, 13; 39; 57; 62 (bottom)

Isabella Ginanneschi/Franca Speranza, srl, 100; 121 (top)

Saharoff/Zeligs/Franca Speranza, srl, 59

Michael Garland, 93

Bill Geddes, 21; 79 (bottom)

Tria Giovan, 19; 86 (bottom)

Steve Gross & Susan Daley, 43; 46; 56; 58; 68; 87; 98; 128; 132

Reto Guntli, 27; 38; 65; 81

Reprinted by Permission from *House Beautiful*, copyright © March 1998. Hearst Communications, Inc. All Rights Reserved. Alexandre Bailhache, photographer, 61; 64; 82

Reprinted by Permission from *House Beautiful*, copyright © December 2000. Hearst Communications, Inc. All Rights Reserved. Anita Calero, photographer, 121 (bottom)

Reprinted by Permission from *House Beautiful*, copyright © July 2000. Hearst Communications, Inc. All Rights Reserved. Oberto Gili, photographer, 107

Reprinted by Permission from *House Beautiful*, copyright © September 2000. Hearst Communications, Inc. All Rights Reserved. Thibeault Jeanson, photographer, 127 (top) (bottom)

Reprinted by Permission from *House Beautiful*, copyright © July 1998. Hearst Communications, Inc. All Rights Reserved. Nedjeljko Matura, photographer, 5; 77; 135

Reprinted by Permission from *House Beautiful*, copyright © December 2000. Hearst Communications, Inc. All Rights Reserved. Lisa Romerein, photographer, 10; 127 (bottom)

Roger Ide, 31

Tim Beddow/The Interior Archive, 51; 125

Fritz von der Schulenberg/The Interior Archive, 89

Henry Wilson/The Interior Archive, 47 (top)

Andrew Wood/The Interior Archive, 75; 114 (bottom); 118

©Jahreszeiten-Verlag/G. Zimmerman, 99

Melba Levick, 90-91

Massimo Listri, 28; 50; 78; 80; 84 (right); 111 (top & bottom); 136

Courtesy of Madison Resort, Golf & Spa, 117 (top)

Lucretia Moroni, 67; 106; 134

Courtesy of Mottahedeh, 26

Novika.com, 69